THE SMILE-HIGH CLUB

Outrageous but True Air Travel Stories

THE SMILE-HIGH CLUB

Outrageous but True Air Travel Stories

**Andrews McMeel
Publishing**

Kansas City

Design by Pete Lippincott

02 03 04 05 06 RR2 10 9 8 7 6 5 4 3 2 1

ISBN: 0-7407-2727-3

Library of Congress Control Number: 2002103635

"In the space age, man will be able to fly around the world in two hours—one hour for flying and one hour to get to the airport.

—NEIL H. MCELROY,
Look, 1958

Contents

The course of the flight up and down was exceedingly erratic, due partly to the irregularity of the air, and partly to lack of experience in handling the machine.

—ORVILLE WRIGHT

The Flying Circus

DELAYED FLIGHTS, missed connections, crowded airports. All of us road warriors have experienced the trials and tribulations of air travel.

But for every overbooked flight, lost bag, or grouchy seat-mate, there's usually an outrageous incident that offers a refreshing breather from the travails of traveling. This book is a collection of hilarious but true moments that have occurred throughout the world of commercial aviation—including in the cockpit, cabin, lavatory, galley, gate area, and control tower.

Among dozens of wacky accounts, you'll read about the Delta captain who thoughtfully had pizza delivered to the 105 passengers stuck on his plane on the tarmac for hours . . . the flight engineer who tumbled out the rear door of a taxiing 727 and chased after the plane . . . the lusty, loud newlyweds whose induction into the Mile-High Club in the lavatory was cheered by passengers . . . the elderly woman who brought her dead husband aboard and flew in first class with him . . . and the drunk who ruined dozens of in-flight meals after he mistook the galley for the lavatory.

To gather these ignoble incidents, we talked to scores of airline personnel, including pilots, flight attendants, passengers, air traffic controllers, gate agents, and baggage handlers. In many cases, usually because of company policy or to avoid embarrassment, our sources asked us to use their first names only, which we agreed to do.

It is hoped that the true, zany stories in this book will help you forget the stale cabin air, the tasteless box lunch, and the cramped legroom of your next flight and in the process lift your mood sky high.

At the Gate

Majority Rules

BEING A GATE AGENT at Washington Dulles International Airport has provided Adria Taylor with an opportunity to meet many of America's elected officials. Some are quite humble; others, unfortunately, have egos the size of the Capitol.

While talking on his cell phone at the gate one day, a gruff congressman handed his ticket to Adria and authoritatively ordered, "Hold this flight. I'm on an important call." Then he rushed away without waiting for a response from her. Adria shook her head in wonderment: *Does he really think we will hold the plane for him?*

While the passengers filed down the jetway, the congressman guardedly talked on his cell phone in the corner of the boarding area. Soon after Adria made a final boarding announcement, the plane's door was closed and the jet backed away from the gate. Finishing his phone call, the congressman turned from his cloistered corner and marched to the check-in counter. "I'm ready to go now," he told Adria as he headed toward the jetway.

Smiling to herself, the gate agent declared, "I'm sorry, sir. The plane has left the gate."

"What?" thundered the congressman. "How could you do that?"

"When the plane was filled, I went on board and told the passengers they were going to participate in good old-fashioned American democracy by getting to vote on the departure time," she said. "One hundred twenty-five of your constituents on board voted to leave on time. Majority rules!"

Pin One On

KEVIN, A SALESMAN, had been on the road and in the air for a full week. He was tired and wanted to go home, but he had encountered several problems with his return reservation. After spending more time on his cell phone with the airlines than he wanted, his difficulties appeared to be corrected.

When he reached the gate in Boise, Idaho, he faced yet another problem with his changed reservation. He lost his composure and went into a tirade for all to witness. "Why hasn't the electronic age come to Boise?" he bellowed.

The counter agent endured Kevin's outburst without showing any emotion herself. She typed a few commands into her computer, and soon all was solved. The electronic age was alive and well in Boise, at least as far as she was concerned. She told Kevin he was booked on the flight and not to worry. Then she asked him to lean forward. "I need to pin this badge on your lapel. Show it to the flight attendant when you board the plane."

Still a bit grumpy from his harangue, Kevin thought maybe he was going to be given some special treatment. After all, he had been through a lot getting a seat on this flight. Following the counter agent's directions, he boarded the plane and went directly to the first flight attendant he saw and showed her his badge. Finally relaxing his demeanor, he asked, "Am I getting an upgrade with this badge?"

"Not really," the flight attendant replied. "Normally, we put this badge on children to identify the ones needing special attention. Looks to me like you've done something at the gate warning us you need to be handled like a child."

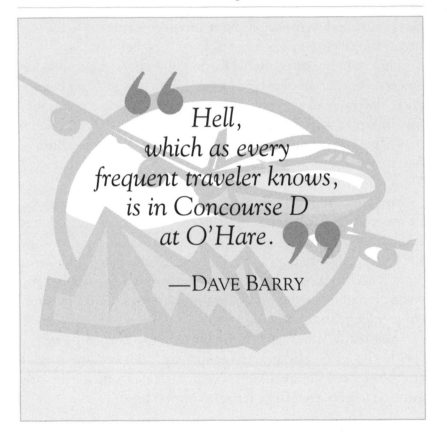

Hell,
which as every
frequent traveler knows,
is in Concourse D
at O'Hare.

—DAVE BARRY

Alphabet Soup

ROAD WARRIOR BRAD ELLIS raced up to the Northwest Airlines gate agent at Minneapolis–St. Paul International Airport and frantically waved his ticket. The agent was just closing the door to the jetway. "Traffic was a monster," he tried to explain. "I hate the freeway and the rental car location. I know I'm late, but could you please get me on this flight?"

The gate agent had heard this lament before from late passengers, but she did her best to quickly give Brad the boarding pass. "You just made it," she told him. "We were closing the door. Tell the first flight attendant you see that you are the 'l-m-n-o-p' and she'll let you on."

"Oh, thanks," the frenzied passenger said as he ran down the jetway, not bothering to ask the agent exactly what all that meant. As Brad stepped onto the Memphis-bound A320 Airbus, he met the onboard leader and told her, "I'm supposed to tell you I'm the 'l-m-n-o-p.'"

"Welcome aboard," the flight attendant told him. "We're about to secure the door, so please take your seat." Once the plane was airborne, Brad summoned the flight attendant and asked, "Just what does 'l-m-n-o-p' mean?"

She giggled and answered, "The letters stand for 'last-minute, never-on-time passenger.'"

Number, Please!

A CONFUSED MIDDLE-AGED MALE passenger stopped flight attendant Justin Amthor in the United Air Lines concourse in Chicago's O'Hare International Airport and said, "Sir, excuse me. Would you mind telling me how to tell which plane to get on?"

Justin asked, "Have you checked in at the gate? What's your flight number?"

Pointing out the terminal window, the confused man told Justin his flight number and said, "None of the planes out there have that number on them."

Identity Crisis

SEVERAL YEARS AGO at Denver's Stapleton Airport, a crowded United Air Lines flight had been canceled. One lonely ticket agent was trying to rebook a long line of angry passengers. Suddenly, one man pushed his way past the others to the desk, slapped his ticket down on the counter, and demanded, "I have to be in first class on the next flight."

Trying to calm the man down by using a soft voice, the ticket agent said, "I'm sorry, but there are other people in line ahead of you. I'm doing the best I can here. I'll help you when it's your turn in line."

Unimpressed with the agent's answer, the man responded, "Do you have any idea who I am?"

Without hesitation, the agent reached for the microphone and announced, "We have a passenger who does not know who he is. If you know him, please come forward and claim him."

Plane Talk

AS A YOUNG WOMAN boarded a plane in Oregon, she casually asked the gate agent something that had been bothering her, "That jet looks kind of small out there. What kind is it?"

"Oh, you'll be flying on a Fokker F-28 today," the gate agent responded.

Said the passenger with a straight face, "Well, I sure hope that little Fokker gets off the ground."

A Revealing Conversation

STEVE, A US AIRWAYS GATE AGENT at Palm Beach International, sensed that he would have a problem as the buxom young blonde approached the counter. First off, all the men in the area were ogling her and all the women were clucking in disdain at her. Steve figured out why once the woman handed him her ticket. She was wearing an extremely short, tight pair of shorts, high heels—and a see-through blouse that clearly showed off her braless, silicone-enhanced breasts.

"Ma'am, I can't let you on the plane in that outfit," he told her.

"Why not?" she asked.

"Well, it's too revealing and distracting. Some of the passengers would find it objectionable."

"Honey," she replied, "I guarantee you no one finds my body objectionable. Men love to look at it and women would love to have it. Besides, what's wrong with a little advertising? I'm a stripper."

"Ma'am, there won't be any peep shows on this flight. Please change into something more suitable—and make sure you do it in the bathroom and not out here."

The stripper reluctantly donned a T-shirt that she had to buy in a terminal shop before she was allowed on the flight.

Pre-board Preferences

THIS DELTA AIR LINES gate announcement in Hartsfield Atlanta International Airport in 1999 had everyone laughing in the boarding area: "Anyone needing special assistance may now board. . . . All those wearing purple babushkas may now board. . . . Would Kenneth Starr please come to the ticket counter. . . . Anyone whose last name ends with the letters X or Z may now board. . . . All those who are at least seven feet tall may now board. . . . Would Monica Lewinsky please come to the ticket counter. . . . Anyone with one green eye and one blue eye may now board . . ."

*If we love to fly
so much,
how come we're in
such a hurry
to get there?*

—LOUIE MANYAK

Just (Para)Chute Me

TAKING HER FIRST FLIGHT, Marilyn Broome expressed her fear of flying to the gate agent. Marilyn had been able to avoid flying for years, but an emergency required her to take a flight back home to Louisiana.

The agent was kind and reassured Marilyn as best she could. When Marilyn hesitated to leave the counter with her boarding pass, the agent, with tongue firmly planted in cheek, said, "Oh, ma'am, I almost forgot to tell you. Go to Gate Three. They'll give you a helmet, scarf, goggles, and a parachute. Then you'll be all set."

Marilyn replied, "Give the pilot the helmet, scarf, and goggles. I'll keep the parachute for myself."

Too Cool

A TWELVE-YEAR-OLD BOY who was flying alone was talking on his cell phone at the gate of his connecting flight at Pittsburgh International Airport. He was overheard saying in his cool grown-up manner: "I had to bury my face in the latest Harry Potter book to get the grandmother type next to me to stop talking. She said I was cute, and she couldn't believe I was flying alone. She even pinched my cheeks and said I reminded her of her grandson. The airline took me to the activity center with all the other 'calves.' What a total bore that was. Bunch of little kids hanging out looking scared. Tell the class I said 'hey' and I'll be back next week."

It'll Make Her Hair Stand on End

THE GATE AGENT at Palm Beach International asked an elderly woman if she wanted a window seat.

"Oh no," replied the woman. "Not by the window. I just had my hair done."

A Lame Excuse

WHEN THE US AIRWAYS GATE AGENT at Philadelphia International Airport gave the preboarding announcement for those passengers needing special assistance, she took notice of a bearded middle-aged man in Bermuda shorts who was using a cane. The man, who wore a unique gold medallion around his neck, limped ahead of the others and boarded early.

Several days later, she was at the gate of a late-arriving flight, directing passengers who were trying to make their connections. One of the disembarking passengers was the bearded man in the Bermuda shorts. Only this time he didn't have a cane, nor was he limping. When she told him the gate for his connecting flight was in the next concourse and leaving in ten minutes, he took off in a mad dash.

A few weeks later, the same man showed up at the gate, but was once again limping with a cane. When it came time to preboard those needing special assistance, there he was, wanting to get on the plane early. The gate agent was no fool. She knew he was using the cane and faking a limp just so he could get a seat ahead of the others.

As she took his ticket, she whispered to him, "Become a frequent flyer and you won't need your cane anymore."

He turned beet red and hobbled down the jetway without saying a word. But he got the message. She never saw him with the cane again.

A Place by Any Other Name

BOB WARTERS, editor of the British magazine *Today's Golfer*, planned to fly from England to the famed Augusta National to cover the 1992 Masters. So he called his travel agent to book him on a flight to Augusta.

Everything went well on the first leg of the journey—a flight from Manchester, England, to Boston. After Bob cleared customs at Boston's Logan International Airport, a friendly airline attendant looked at his ticket and pointed him to a nearby gate.

When Bob boarded the plane, he was a bit concerned because it was a prop and not a jet. *Props are for short commuter hops*, he thought. *Augusta is more than a thousand miles away. Oh, well, maybe the airline is cutting back on its service.*

But Bob became more concerned after the plane took off. He looked out the window and noticed something wasn't right. *The ocean is on my right side, not my left*, he told himself. *I don't know why we're heading north. Maybe it's just some quirk in the traffic pattern. Hopefully, before long the pilot will turn around and get headed in the right direction.*

But then the plane landed. Bob looked at his watch and noticed he had been in the air for only fifty minutes. The flight on a jetliner should have taken two hours. Something definitely wasn't right.

Bob went into the terminal and in his British accent asked the gate agent, "Is this Augusta, Georgia?"

"No," came the reply. "This is Augusta, Maine."

Aghast, Bob hustled to the ticket counter, where he learned his travel agent had given him a ticket to the wrong Augusta. Bob had to spend the night in Maine plus pay several hundred dollars for a new plane ticket. But eventually he made it to the right Augusta in time to cover the Masters.

Better Late Than Never

ED, A VICE PRESIDENT for a frozen seafood company, traveled extensively by air. Dubbed the "Flying Colonel," he had all the perks that frequent flyers are awarded, including first-class upgrades. He also was accustomed to flying repeatedly to the same major cities. Because he was so familiar with the usual gates at the various airports that he frequented, he rarely looked at the monitors to determine at which gate his departing plane would be.

One afternoon, he was flying to San Diego via a connection to give a presentation to an important client the following day. Ed had decided to take a flight the day before the meeting, just to make sure he had plenty of time. With his connecting flight arriving late into Albuquerque, he had to run to his next gate. Panicked that he was going to miss his connection, he did not take time to check the monitor or ask an airline official which gate he was supposed to go to. After all, he had taken this flight many times in the past. He reasoned to himself, *No need to waste time looking at the monitor. I've got to run.*

Winded from sprinting, Ed reached the gate just before the agent was about to close it. The agent quickly tore off the stub of the ticket and motioned Ed to get on board, where he found his seat in first class. He ordered a drink from the flight attendant and settled back to await the takeoff. When the flight attendant made the announcements over the public address system, Ed didn't pay any attention to what she was saying.

As the plane made the turn on the runway for takeoff, the man next to Ed looked at his watch and said, "We're getting off right on time. I thought I'd be late, but it looks like I'll get to Boston right on time."

"Boston?" Ed questioned. "Don't you mean San Diego?"

"No," the passenger replied. "This is Flight 1132 to Boston."

Poor Ed. He had been in such a rush in Albuquerque that he hadn't checked the gate number for his flight to San Diego. The gate for the San Diego flight was adjacent to the one for the Boston flight. Because Ed had arrived so late, the gate agent failed to check his first-class ticket thoroughly.

Ed had to spend the night on the wrong coast. The following morning, he started out on his trip west again. Only this time, he carefully checked the gate of his departure. After a pleasant nonstop flight to San Diego, he arrived four hours late for his presentation and apologized profusely.

"It took a lot of guts to show up late," the customer told him, "so I felt I should meet you."

Because the joke was on Ed, the important customer had a good laugh and forgave him for his tardiness. Boosted by a good night's sleep, Ed made a great presentation and closed the deal.

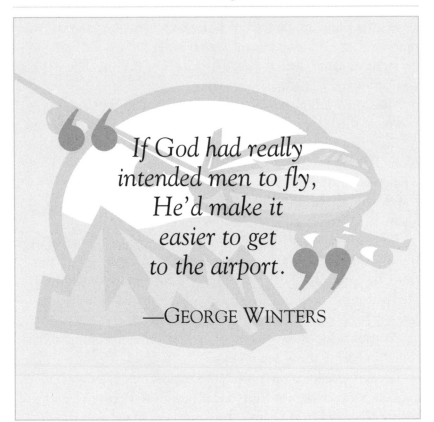

If God had really intended men to fly, He'd make it easier to get to the airport.

—GEORGE WINTERS

Mo' Money

AT AN INTERNATIONAL GATE in Frankfurt, Germany, the gate agent stated over the public address system, "If you are carrying more than ten thousand dollars in currency, you must fill out a declaration form. The plane will be leaving in fifteen minutes for Lagos, Nigeria."

A passenger asked the agent, "I have forty thousand dollars with me. May I just divide it between my three friends so I don't have to declare it? Each of them could carry ten thousand dollars."

Because he was honest, he had to file forms with the government.

Sleepless Since Seattle

IN A REAL-LIFE VERSION of the hit movie *Sleepless in Seattle*, two "almost airborne" souls found each other and true love.

It began in 1994 with a brief encounter in a lounge area at Seattle-Tacoma International Airport. Barry Aurich, thirty, was waiting for a commuter flight back to his home in Eugene,

Oregon. Rita Weddle, thirty-two, was also in the lounge waiting for her return commuter flight to Yakima, Washington.

"He smiled and started chatting with me in a friendly way, and I was caught up in the conversation," recalled Rita, a traveling sales representative who had never been married. "We talked about hobbies, travel, everything under the sun. I felt like we had been friends forever."

Although Barry was engrossed in their conversation, he didn't want to miss his plane, so he reluctantly ended their engaging fifteen-minute chat and left to catch his flight. "He turned back and gave me a smile," Rita recalled. "When he was gone, I missed him."

Once Barry was settled in the plane, he kept thinking, *I've been looking for you for so long. Am I ever going to see you again?* His short flight to Eugene left him unsettled because he couldn't keep that sweet woman out of his mind. He just had to see her again. But in his rush from the lounge to catch his plane, he had failed to learn one important detail about Rita—he had forgotten to get her name.

So the next morning, he wrote an ad for placement in her town's newspaper. The ad in the *Yakima Herald-Republic* read: "Sleepless since Seattle! I left without getting even her name. Please help me find a woman I met at Sea-Tac Airport Tuesday night. She moved back to Yakima a year ago after living in Boston for five years. She's thirty-two, tall, slender, light brown/blonde straight hair, brown eyes, has several dogs and cats, never been married, and works in the financial planning field. If you know who she is, please have her call Barry in Eugene." The ad included his phone number.

Coincidentally, the day the ad appeared, a friend of Rita's saw it and immediately called her. Rita was stunned. "I couldn't believe Barry was as attracted to me as I was to him," she recalled. The stars had gotten into both their eyes. "I phoned my mom asking for advice. She said, 'Go for it. He sounds like one in a million.'"

With her mother's blessing, Rita called Barry the next day. They soon were gabbing almost every day long-distance until an airliner brought Rita to Barry. They took a camping trip together and fell in love.

"We talked until dawn under the stars and decided we couldn't live without each other," gleamed Rita. Less than three months later, they were married.

A Wing and a Prayer

DAVE AND LAURA QUIGLEY wed in Hawaii—after surviving a scare at the gate.

The couple, neither of whom had been married before, met while scuba diving when they were in their forties. After they fell in love, they selected a grotto on the Hawaiian island of Kauai as the perfect spot for their wedding. It wouldn't be that expensive because Laura, an employee of a major airline, could fly free as a "non-rev" (non-revenue-paying) passenger and her fiancé could go on a "buddy pass." Dave liked to joke with friends that he was "marrying a pass."

As their wedding day approached, Dave sat Laura down in order to make a schedule and finalize all the wedding plans. He wanted to clarify times and places with her so everything would go smoothly. Dave was the detail-oriented person in the relationship and was also the one who did all the worrying.

Dave and Laura agreed to meet at the airport gate an hour before the flight. Dave arrived on time as usual, wait-listed with the gate agent, and found a seat in the empty waiting area. Eventually other passengers began to arrive, and the seats in the gate area filled with excited travelers. But Laura wasn't one of them yet. Twinges of concern started to creep into Dave's mind the longer he waited for her. *Where is she?* he asked himself. *She definitely should have been here by now. Did she get into an accident? Did she get cold feet?* Easing his worries, the gate agent confirmed Laura was on the "non-rev" list and she would probably get a seat with her seniority.

Soon passengers began boarding the plane. No Laura. Standby passengers then boarded, including Dave. Still, no Laura. Close to hyperventilating in his seat, Dave left the plane and asked the gate agent again if her name appeared on the list. "Yes. Sir, you need to take your seat on the plane because we're preparing to close the door." It was a tough decision, but Dave reluctantly decided to reboard the plane, especially since he was lucky to get a seat with his buddy pass. The gate agent followed Dave and closed the door to the aircraft.

In the meantime, Laura had taken her sweet time leaving home and casually drove to the airport. *After all,* she thought, *I always leave home one hour before the flight. I park in the employee lot and always have time to spare*. But luck was not with her today. Traffic snarled around the airport, and a stream of cars battled for a few open spaces in the employee parking lot. Laura's stomach began to tighten. She finally parked, grabbed her suitcase, and rushed through the terminal.

Running down the concourse, she noticed that no one was at the gate. Although the door to the jetway was closed, it wasn't locked. She raced down the jetway only to see the cabin door on the airplane was closed. She turned to the jetway window and, with hands folded in a praying position, looked into the pilot's eyes, begging him to reopen the cabin. "Please let me in!" she yelled. "Please! I'm getting married!"

The sympathetic crew in the cockpit ordered the flight attendants to open the door and let Laura board. Minutes later, Laura was enjoying a mimosa in first class while Dave sat squished between two women in coach. But he didn't mind too much. After all, his bride-to-be had made it onto the plane on a wing and a prayer.

*If God
wanted us to fly,
He would have
given us tickets.*

—MEL BROOKS

Sympathy Pains

AMERICAN PASSENGER Mitch Glisan found out just how much of a pain traveling can be, especially in a foreign country.

He was listed on an Aerolineas Argentinas flight from Buenos Aires, Argentina, to São Paulo, Brazil. But after standing one hour in line at the gate to receive his boarding pass for the flight, he was shocked to hear this announcement: "Due to the fact that the crews of our national airline are now on strike, we ground staff have joined them in a vote of confidence. We are proclaiming a sympathy strike tonight. If you want to fly to São Paulo, it won't be on this airline. You'll need to wait in line at the Varig counter if you want to get a flight tonight or tomorrow morning."

Two hundred passengers stormed the Varig Airlines gate agent only to wait another hour in another line. After two frustrating hours, the passengers had lost their sympathy for any cause at the Buenos Aires airport.

Meanwhile, Varig put a 727 in service. The gate agent then led two hundred people, all carrying their own luggage, down the backstairs and through the bowels of the airport.

Once outside on the tarmac, the passengers were told to toss all of their luggage—none of which was tagged—into an old beat-up pickup truck. The passengers couldn't help but wonder if they would ever see their bags again.

Happy to be headed to São Paulo, the weary travelers climbed the rear stairway of the plane, which already had its jet engines roaring. Once on board, Mitch suggested to his fellow tired passengers, mostly Americans, "Let's have a pool to see how many bags we think will make it to São Paulo." He passed a sheet of paper around the plane and passengers made their guesses. Betting seemed to cheer them up.

Surprisingly, no bags were lost on the flight to São Paulo. "I guess my sympathy pains went away once we knew everybody got all their luggage," Mitch said at the baggage claim area. Meanwhile, the most optimistic of the passengers walked off with the winnings of the pool.

Gunning for Trouble

FOR SOME GUYS, getting even is worth taking a chance.

Grant and his buddies at a Springfield, Illinois, company that made electric meters worked for a man who made it difficult for anyone to like him. As the boss, he was unapproachable, opinionated, and sharp-tongued. His underlings took his orders and tried to stay out of his way. So it came as no surprise when one of the guys had an idea to sabotage the boss.

In the company shop, the engineers cut a piece of sheet metal into the shape of a gun. Then, while the boss was out to lunch, they sneaked into his office and "borrowed" his Samsonite briefcase. Inside the briefcase flap, they sliced a small opening and placed the flat fake gun in it. They returned the briefcase to its place in his closet.

The following week, the boss left on a business trip. Later on the phone with his secretary, he told her what happened to him during a security check at the airport. "When I put the briefcase through the X-ray machine, a small handgun showed on the screen. I told the security officer I didn't have a gun, but they ripped my briefcase apart. There it was! I had no idea how it got there. I ended up missing my plane. Tell the guys we're going to have a department meeting when I get back. I'll be gunning for the culprit who did this to me."

Case of the Missing Stroller

A COUPLE IN THEIR LATE TWENTIES traveling with their four-month-old baby patiently waited for the DC-9 passengers to deplane at Los Angeles International Airport. When the cabin was nearly empty, the young father reached in the overhead compartment for the stroller. It was the small collapsible type, just big enough to hold the baby and small enough to negotiate through an airport with baby and diaper bag. To his dismay, it wasn't where he thought he'd placed it, so he and his wife checked all the other overhead compartments, but to no avail.

Confused by the missing stroller, he then sought the help of flight attendant Marilyn Ingham. After a thorough search, Marilyn declared the carry-on stroller "missing." Holding the baby's diaper bag, she escorted the couple and their baby down the concourse. Naturally, the discussion revolved around the strange disappearance of the stroller: "Who would want it? Why would anyone deliberately take it? How could anyone accidentally take it?" They couldn't understand it.

Suddenly, Marilyn noticed a man from their flight pushing a stroller several yards ahead of them. They quickened their pace in order to catch up with the passenger and the stroller. Unbelievably, there in the stroller sat a large, bulky watermelon. After they confronted him, the man explained he was personally delivering the watermelon to an old friend in Los Angeles. Because the watermelon was so awkward to carry, he thought he would use the stroller to push it through the crowded airport.

"I just thought the stroller was free for passengers to use like pillows and blankets," he explained.

"Well, it's not," said Marilyn. "You should know better than to borrow someone else's stroller."

The relieved couple, happy to have their stroller returned, buckled the baby and disappeared into the crowd at LAX. Holding the heavy watermelon in his arms, the man whined to Marilyn, "Now, what am I supposed to do with this watermelon?"

Marilyn wanted to tell him. Oh, how she wanted to tell him.

In the Cockpit

Shiny Switches

FIRST OFFICER KEITH SPILLMAN was sitting in the cockpit of a DC-9 waiting for the passengers to board, when a woman stuck her head in the open door. She appeared quite concerned. "Do you know what all those dials and switches do?" she inquired.

Thinking she must be joking, he answered, "No, I only touch the shiny switches so I know I won't get in trouble. Those are the ones we use all the time."

Zoom. Out of the cockpit, up the jetway she ran with Spillman following behind her. The frowning gate agent met Keith at the counter and grumbled, "Thanks a lot. We had spent almost an hour trying to convince her it was safe to fly. We had told her to have a look at the cockpit and talk to the crew for reassurance. You sure took care of her!"

Even the promise of a seat in first class wouldn't lure the woman back onto the plane.

If black boxes
survive air crashes,
then why don't
they make
the whole plane
out of that stuff?

—GEORGE CARLIN

Turning the Other Cheek

ALTHOUGH IT MAY SOUND STRANGE, quite often members of
the flight crew have never worked together as a team and may
never work together again. Each person bids for his or her
schedule on a monthly basis. Depending on seniority and
desired flights, the crew members may never see each other
again. So if there is an issue between any of them, they usually
resolve it while they are together or else let it pass.

During one 4-hour flight on an L-1011, the copilot kept
expelling gas much to the discomfort of his fellow crew members. Cramped in small quarters, it was difficult to concentrate
with the foul fumes floating through the air. After the gagging
flight, the captain told the engineer he was going to spend the
evening on their layover eating "revenge food." The following
morning, the three officers took their seats in the cockpit for
the return flight.

Turning to the copilot, the captain said, "Remember how
you passed gas all day yesterday? Well, I'm about to get even
with you. Listen to this one." The captain then leaned on his
left rear cheek and grunted. Instead of foul air coming from

his body, as he expected, bodily waste squirted out, covering the seat of his pants and streaming down his right leg.

The mortified pilot gingerly walked off the plane, rinsed his pants in the crew lounge, and put on a new pair. The L-1011 left thirty minutes late. After that experience, the captain decided never to seek revenge on a person he probably would never see again. His new philosophy was "Let it go." But then, that's sort of what he did.

Shifting the Blame

A WOMAN APPROACHED the first officer as she exited the Delta Air Lines flight and gave him an earful: "I happen to fly all the time, and I know all about planes. This was the roughest, worst flight I've ever been on. Whoever was flying this plane doesn't know anything! Every time he shifted, I was thrown forward. He needs to go back to training."

Overhearing her rant, the captain, who had fifteen years' experience, stepped out of the cockpit and apologized to her. "It won't happen again," he assured her. "They're changing all our planes to automatic."

Heaven Help Him

A PIOUS, OVERWEIGHT CAPTAIN wore a belt buckle with "I love Jesus" on it. As two nuns walked onto the plane, he stepped out of the cockpit to greet them. "Sisters, I have something to show you." He lifted up his stomach to proudly show them his belt buckle.

Their reaction was hardly what he had expected. "Oh my! Oh my!" gasped the nuns, covering their eyes. One of the nuns turned to hurry to her seat, but she twisted her ankle and fell in the aisle. The perplexed captain bent over to help her, but she averted her eyes and kept shouting, "Oh my! Oh my!"

Only then did the bewildered pilot look down and realize for the first time that his pants were unzipped and gaping wide open.

Horrified that he had forgotten to zip his fly after a trip to the lavatory, the red-faced captain zipped it up and scurried off. But he didn't hide in the cockpit. Instead, he quickly left the plane. He was so humiliated that he refused to fly the plane. The airlines had to find another captain and put an end to the "nunsense."

I'm Your Captain

WHILE SITTING AT THE GATE ready to back away in the buttoned-up American Airlines 757, the passengers were treated over the PA to the captain's rendition of Grand Funk Railroad's hit tune "I'm Your Captain."

> *Everybody, listen to me.*
> *I'm your captain,*
> *I'm Captain Shane,*
> *And I'm feeling really sane.*
>
> *Everybody, listen to me.*
> *I've been flying this big old plane,*
> *And it's been minutes since I've seen the gate.*
> *Can you hear me?*
>
> *I am not alone.*
> *I've got a copilot whose name is Stime.*
> *If you sit down, we'll get you home on time,*
> *Where you can kiss Mother Earth.*

But first, buckle up in your place.
You'd better think about it.
Am I in my cabin dreaming?
I see everybody's smiling face.

I guess it's time to leave the gate.
Please, Control Tower, don't make us wait.
We're getting you closer to your home.
We're getting you closer to your home.

A huge applause and cheers occurred as he finished this amazing song. "That took a lot of guts," responded the copilot on the PA. "You will *never* catch me doing that!"

Fear Factor

A US AIRWAYS CAPTAIN with a great sense of humor was asked by the airline to confine his one-liners to off-duty hours after he unintentionally made some skittish passengers even more jittery than they already were.

Before the flight, a passenger had stopped by the cockpit and told the pilot, "I'm so afraid to fly."

The captain had nodded knowingly and said, "I know how you feel. I am, too."

Later, during the flight, the plane hit some rough air, so the captain got on the PA and told the passengers, "Forgive me for all the bumps we're experiencing. I'm just learning to fly."

Wake-Up Call

AFTER A LATE NIGHT, Captain Rob dragged himself to the airport for a 6:30 A.M. flight. He showed up an hour before flight time and took his place in the cockpit of the 727.

The captain, copilot, and flight engineer went through their checklists while the passengers boarded the plane. Following instructions from ground contol, the captain told the "push man" (tow operator) that the plane was "clear to push" (ready to be towed), but only after three other planes had left the gate area—a delay that could take up to five minutes.

Having that wonderful ability to fall asleep anywhere and at any time, Captain Rob then dozed off.

Minutes later, the pilot was jolted out of his morning nap when the voice of the "push man" announced through the pilot's headset, "Clear to start!" Seeing the plane moving, the suddenly awakened Captain Rob instinctively slammed on the brakes. The tow bar on the tug pushing the plane snapped when the plane came to a screeching and unexpected halt. The snapped tow bar then popped into the air and smashed into the plane's underbelly.

The passengers weren't too happy when they had to disembark and wait at another gate for a different plane—one without a hole underneath the cockpit.

Captain Rob complained to his first officer, "Next time we fly together, get me some coffee and keep me awake at the gate. I don't want any more wake-up calls like the one I had today!"

A Chance Remark

AN AMERICA WEST AIRLINES FLIGHT from Seattle arrived at McCarran International Airport in Las Vegas two hours late.

As the passengers prepared to deplane, the pilot got on the PA and said, "For those of you visiting Las Vegas, we wish you good luck. And for those of you hoping to make connections, we wish *you* even more good luck."

The pilot is always giving us stupid information. 'If there's anything we can do to make your trip more comfortable, . . .' How about that first-class seat up there? No one's sitting in it.

—GEORGE WALLACE

Take Me Out to the Ball Game

AFTER EVERYBODY HAD BOARDED a Northwest Airlines flight from Detroit to New York's LaGuardia Airport, Captain Greg Arnold told his passengers on the PA, "I regret to inform you that there's a weather delay in New York. Air traffic control won't release us yet. I know how annoying this must be for you, but there is a silver lining in this for me, because I'll be able to find out how my nine-year-old son, Dylan, is doing in his baseball game in Miami."

Fifteen minutes later, Greg dialed his cell phone from the cockpit and called his wife, Renée, who was at the game, for an update. Then he got on the PA and informed his passengers that ATC was still holding the plane. "And, oh yes, my son Dylan doubled and scored a run in the first inning. It's now the bottom of the second and the Cardinals—Dylan's team—are winning two to one."

After another fifteen minutes, Greg called Renée again and then informed his passengers, "Well, we're still stuck here, but hopefully they'll release us soon. On a better note, Dylan drove in a run in the third inning with a single, and the

Cardinals are now ahead four to two at the end of four innings." Some of the passengers clapped.

Finally, the plane took off and landed an hour late in New York. When Greg stepped out of the cockpit to say good-bye to the passengers, he was met by the first person to disembark. The person stopped and asked the captain, "So, how did the game turn out?"

"Yeah," said another passenger, "who won?"

Greg pulled out his cell phone and called his wife. After learning the results, he smiled, turned to the passengers, and said, "The Cardinals won six to two. Dylan was three for three." He had to repeat the happy results for dozens of other deplaning passengers who wanted to know how Dylan's team did.

Wing Walking

FROM A WISECRACKING SOUTHWEST AIRLINES PILOT to the passengers: "Folks, we have reached our cruising altitude now, so I am going to switch the seat belt sign off. Feel free to move about as you wish, but please stay inside the plane till we land. It's a bit cold outside."

Hold That Flight!

THE FLASHING LIGHT on the control panel warned the flight crew of an unlocked stairway located in the rear of the Delta Air Lines 727. They would not be cleared for takeoff while it kept blinking. So Dennis, the flight engineer, was sent to check the lock while the full plane taxied onto the runway at Tulsa International Airport.

He pushed on the back door, fumbled with the lock, and finally slammed his hip into it. Boom! The door opened unexpectedly. Losing his balance, Dennis tumbled through the open door and rolled down the stairs, out the back end of the plane, which was continuing to taxi toward the takeoff position.

Scrambling to his feet, the slightly bruised flight engineer ran after the 727, yelling and waving as if the pilot could actually hear or see him. Of course, no one heard him, but someone did see him

An American Airlines plane was directly behind the frantic engineer. Fortunately for Dennis, the American pilot radioed the Delta pilot: "You'd better slow down. Your engineer is trying to catch the flight."

The startled pilot slowed the plane to a stop, and Dennis ran back up the rear stairs. He reentered the cabin, pulled the door shut, and calmly walked to the front of the plane. He took his place in the cockpit, where the light no longer blinked. Mission accomplished.

Dennis looked over at the captain and said, "Hey, thanks for waiting for me."

"No problem," answered the captain. "I like you."

No Respect

FROM A PILOT during his welcome message: "We are pleased to have some of the best flight attendants in the industry. Unfortunately, none of them is on this flight."

Wild Ride

AS THE PLANE WAS COMING to a stop after landing at a faster speed than usual at Washington's Reagan National Airport, a lone voice came over the PA: "Whoa, big fella. Whoa!"

Courtesy Lights

ON A BRAZILIAN COMMUTER FLIGHT on Nordeste Airlines, frequent flyer Ben Bugara was invited by the pilot to ride in the jump seat in the cockpit. (Apparently, Nordeste has a more liberal cockpit policy than most other airlines.)

Much of the view was obscured by smoke from slash-and-burn clearing of fields below. As the plane approached Valadares, a cliff appeared through the cloud of smoke. Immediately, the pilot began turning the plane's lights on and off.

"Why are you flicking the lights?" Ben asked.

"I'm warning the hang gliders jumping off the cliff to stop while we pass over," the Brazilian pilot answered. "I always give them a warning so our turbulence doesn't cause them trouble and mess up their gliding."

Out of the Mouths of Babes

VETERAN PILOT PAUL WENSKE enjoyed showing a little six-year-old girl the flight deck. He had a daughter about the same age at home and knew how excited kids get when shown the cockpit with all its controls.

Like other children her age, the little girl was thrilled. As she ran back through first class to her mom, she stopped, turned around, and yelled, "Captain Paul, please don't kill us in the airplane today."

Say Good Night, Kids

FLYING OVER RURAL KANSAS in a jetliner one fall evening was a delightful experience for passenger Walt Morris as he watched the twinkling farmhouse lights below. Suddenly, the serenity of the evening was broken when the plane's landing lights started flashing on and off.

What's happening? he wondered as he clenched the arm-rests. As the pilot came on the PA to make an announcement, Morris thought, *This is it. He's going to tell us we've got a major problem.*

Instead, the captain told the passengers, "In case you are worried about the flashing lights outside the plane, I am blinking an acknowledgment to my kids. They are at home over on that hill to the left, and they just sent me a Morse code message saying, "Good night, Dad.'"

Delivering Good Service

CAPTAINS ARE OFTEN WILLING to go that extra mile to placate their passengers during unexpected delays. For example, two Delta Air Lines pilots ordered fast food during delays in 1999, according to *USA Today*.

To keep his Cincinnati-bound passengers and their stomachs from grumbling too much during a long delay in Albany, New York, Captain Scott Robertson walked to a McDonald's inside the terminal and ordered 100 hamburgers and 50 bags of fries. Then, remembering the need to treat first-class passengers with extra service, Robertson went next door to Pizza Hut and ordered 12 pan pizzas.

A couple of months earlier, Delta pilot John Johnson phoned for forty cheese pizzas after a pressurization problem forced an unexpected late-night setdown in Amarillo, Texas.

Johnson's tab ran $380, including a midnight run to a Wal-Mart for a mother who had run out of baby food.

When a Chicago-bound United Air Lines jet was diverted to Minneapolis–St. Paul International Airport to wait out a snowstorm in 2000, the 105 passengers remained on the plane, getting frustrated and hungry.

Captain Tim Claiborne knew he had to do something soon or else face a possible cabin revolt like those that erupted on several Northwest Airlines planes when passengers were stranded on board—with no food and overflowing toilets—for up to eight hours during a blizzard in Detroit in 1999.

So Claiborne phoned a local Domino's Pizza from the cockpit and ordered fifteen jumbo pizzas—some with pepperoni, some plain—to be brought to the rear stairs so his sullen passengers could get fed. He paid with his personal credit card. The mood in the cabin lightened considerably after the flight attendants passed out slices of pizza served on cocktail napkins.

Said one contented passenger, "This sure beats regular airplane food."

*In the early days,
they said I was trying to
make a statement,
but I was trying to
make a living.*

—CAPTAIN BONNIE TIBURZI,
first woman pilot hired by a major airline

Who Loves Ya, Baby?

FROM A SOUTHWEST AIRLINES PILOT to the passengers: "Weather at our destination is sixty-five degrees with some broken clouds, but we'll try to have them fixed before we arrive. Thank you. Remember, nobody loves ya, baby, or loves your money, more than Southwest."

Unlucky Thirteen

"WELCOME ABOARD Trans World Airlines Flight 236 from Little Rock to Kansas City," Captain Patrick announced to his passengers. "Today we are having a contest for a free washer and dryer. Please write your seat number on a slip of paper and give it to the flight attendant. We'll announce the winner later in the flight."

The passengers clapped while the flight crew laughed to themselves. They knew what the winner would actually take home.

After the slips of paper were collected, they were discarded. The captain then picked a number at random in his head. He chose number thirteen because it was the thirteenth of the month. "Hi, folks. This is Captain Patrick," he told the passengers. "Congratulations to the person in 13C. You are TWA's lucky winner today. Stay seated and our flight attendant will bring you the prize."

Lucky seat 13C received a rubber plumbing washer and a paper towel. Rather than taking the joke good-naturedly, the winner filed a formal complaint upon deplaning. He didn't think the contest was funny. He had felt insulted and humiliated because the rest of the passengers on the plane had laughed at him. Captain Patrick was reprimanded and had to write an official apology to the gentleman.

A New Meaning for the Word *Cockpit*

ONE LATE NIGHT the flight crew of an Eastern Airlines plane decided to have some fun with the voice recorder. The device keeps track of anything that's said in the cockpit on a thirty-minute loop. It's especially scrutinized when there is a crash.

The cockpit crew decided that when they were landing the plane, the copilot would shout, "Wow, look at those tentacles!" Due to hot summer weather, Flight 716 had been a bumpy one and anything but boring as the crew had skillfully dodged several storms. On their descent into Phoenix, it became extremely choppy.

Approximately 250 feet from landing, the copilot yelled, "Wow, look at those testicles!"

Fortunately, they landed safely, and no one ever had to replay the voice recorder from that flight, to the relief of the first officer.

You Get What You Pay For

EASTERN AIRLINES L-1011 jet service often offered cheap fares on late-night travel several decades ago. For seventy-nine dollars, the passengers could purchase a one-way ticket from New York to Los Angeles. It was a great deal for travelers on a budget.

On one particular flight, the plane was evading fierce storms all night and battling heavy turbulence before landing safely at its destination.

An extremely angry woman stopped at the cockpit and accosted the flight engineer. "This is the worst flight I've ever been on," she complained. "You had the seat-belt light on almost all night. I could barely smoke my cigarette. My hand kept moving up and down. I want to speak to the captain."

"Well, ma'am, how much did you pay for your ticket?"

"Seventy-nine dollars."

"Well, for anything under two hundred dollars, you get to talk to me. For two hundred to two hundred and fifty, you get to talk to the copilot. And for two hundred and fifty to three hundred, you get to talk to the captain."

After hearing that, the captain turned around from his seat and said, "Lady, we're all lucky to be alive after what we've been through tonight. If I were you, I'd be thanking us for saving your life."

"Yes," added the flight engineer, "how much do you think that's worth?"

Anti-Aircraft Fire

AFTER A PARTICULARLY HARD LANDING in Tampa, the pilot apologized over the PA, and then the crew stood at the door to say good-bye to the passengers as they deplaned. The pilot felt so bad about the landing that he couldn't look anyone in the eye.

None of the passengers said anything derogatory until a sweet little old lady walking with the help of a cane approached him. "Sonny," she said right in his face, "did we land or were we shot down?"

And a Child Shall Lead

THE PILOT'S ANNOUNCEMENT to passengers as the United Air Lines 777 taxied on the John F. Kennedy International Airport runway stated seriously, "If anybody on board knows how to play Microsoft's Flight Simulator, please notify a flight attendant. We need some help up here. In the meantime, sit back and enjoy the flight today, folks."

Passengers looked around wondering if the pilot was kidding. Ten-year-old Zachary Norton assumed there must be some trouble in the cockpit that only knowledge of Flight Simulator could fix. Turning to his mother, Kay, Zachary said, "Mom, I know how to play that one. I'm going up to help the pilot." Before Kay could stop him, he unbuckled his seat belt and trotted toward the cockpit. However, he was stopped by the flight attendant in first class.

"You must go back to your seat. We're about to take off," she told him.

"But the pilot asked for help. I know how to play Flight Simulator. How can we take off without my help?"

"Everything is fine in the cockpit," she assured him. She then explained that the copilot had just purchased the new computer game while on his layover in New York and wanted someone to show him "the ins and outs" of it before giving it as a Christmas present.

About an hour into the flight during a crew break, the copilot visited Zachary, who shared all his expertise of Flight Simulator.

A Voice from Above

YEARS AGO, flight crews often didn't behave quite as professionally as they do now.

Late-night cross-country flights could get a bit boring. Once the passengers' stomachs were full, the movie was over, and the lights were dimmed in the cabin, the service crew would occasionally seek a little diversion.

A former Eastern Airlines flight attendant recalled having fun talking to truckers over their CBs from the cockpit high frequency radio as the plane flew over the vast expanses of the western plains. Here's a typical exchange:

"How fast are you going?" she'd ask a trucker.

"Oh, about seventy."

"That's nothing. I'm going six times faster than that."

"No way!"

"I'll show you."

"Where are you?"

"Look up and you'll see me." She would then signal the pilot to flash the outside lights.

"I guess you don't get any speeding tickets up there, do you?"

Flight reservations systems decide whether or not you exist. If your information isn't in their database, then you simply don't get to go anywhere.

—ARTHUR MILLER

Mood Lighting

ON A NIGHT FLIGHT, the pilot jokingly but thoughtlessly told the passengers, "Ladies and gentlemen, we've reached cruising altitude and will be turning down the cabin lights. This is for your comfort and to enhance the appearance of your flight attendants."

Needless to say, by the time his dinner was served, it was as cold as his remark.

Coneheads

DURING A COAST-TO-COAST RED-EYE Eastern Airlines flight several years ago, the cockpit crew decided to be creative with the aluminum foil that covered individual food trays. Captain John removed the aluminum foil from his dinner and made space helmets for himself and his first officer. Even though they looked ridiculous, it made them laugh. He had enough foil to make four cone-shaped helmets.

Being the practical joker, the captain took the laugh one step further. On the layover in San Francisco, he typed an official-looking notice advising all crew members to wear new ozone protection cones over the Midwest because the ozone layer was opening up there.

Captain John dispensed the "official" notice to his crew when they met the following day for their next flight. Basically, it stated that the ozone layer over Nebraska, Kansas, and Iowa was being depleted at an alarmingly fast rate. Management was deeply concerned over the scientific discovery. Because of the research findings, management was asking all flight crews to don the foil helmets over the Midwest. It was a voluntary decision by each employee, but it was strongly recommended they follow this new procedure until further notice.

Somewhere over Nebraska, the captain buzzed one of the flight attendants for coffee. When she entered the cockpit, she saw all three officers wearing the ozone cones. She handed the captain his coffee, and he gave her a cone. Because she was such a diligent, cautious young lady, she had already decided to follow management's request.

"As you can see, we're complying with the new edict," the captain told the flight attendant. "Who would have thought they cared about the depletion of the ozone layer?"

She put on the cone helmet and as she walked out of the cockpit, the captain announced on the PA: "Please notice our flight attendant modeling Eastern Airline's new ozone helmet as she walks through the cabin. This was especially designed for flying over the Midwest, where the ozone is the thinnest. She'll be taking orders for the helmets."

After her promenade, the flight attendant returned to the cockpit, where the guys informed her of the truth. There was no official Eastern Airlines edict and no ozone-layer problem. They confessed, "We needed a distraction and thought of this idea."

After she thought a minute, her face broke into a smile. "I have the last laugh, Captain. You'll have to tell the passengers to cancel their orders."

Pilots' Words of Wisdom

- Passengers prefer old experienced captains and young inexperienced flight attendants.

- There are four ways to fly—the right way, the wrong way, the company way, and the captain's way. Only one counts.

- Any pilot who doesn't consider himself or herself the best in the game is in the wrong game.

- Since deregulation, matched luggage means three shopping bags from a discount store.

- A smooth touchdown in a simulator is like kissing your sister.

- If the weather is lousy where you are, it's probably great where you're going.

- A good simulator ride is like successful surgery on a cadaver.

In the Cabin

Pretakeoff Takeoff

JIM, A TWENTY-THREE-YEAR-OLD FLIGHT ENGINEER, was still a bit nervous during his first week on the job, especially as he worked alongside seasoned veterans in the cockpit. By the end of the week, he felt much more confident until . . .

As the DC-8 waited in a long line for takeoff, a flight attendant entered the cockpit. Laughing while trying to act serious, she said, "Captain, we have a woman in seat 14C who is taking off her clothes. She's in the aisle, and we've tried to get her to put her clothes on and sit down. She absolutely refuses to listen to any of us. And I can smell alcohol on her."

"Well, send her up to see us," the captain joked. Then, turning to his rookie flight engineer, he said, "Hey, Jim, this is your lucky day. Go back there and take care of her."

So, with visions of an unclad sexy vixen, Jim unbuckled his seat belt, put on his hat, and entered the cabin. Sure enough, standing in the aisle was a woman in bra and panties—an overweight woman old enough to be Jim's mother.

"Please get dressed, ma'am, and have a seat," he said firmly. "We are concerned for your safety. We can't take off until everyone is seated."

Suddenly, the woman threw her arms around the engineer, causing him to lose his balance. They both tumbled into the aisle, where she landed on top of him. He tried to squirm free, but she was too heavy.

"Please let me up," he begged.

"Not until you buy me a drink, Sonny."

"Okay, I'll buy you any drink you want if you get dressed and sit down," the now totally mortified flight engineer promised, scrambling to his feet as the passengers burst out laughing.

Shaking from the ordeal, Jim returned to the cockpit.

"Everything under control?" the captain asked him.

"Yes," replied Jim, still red from embarrassment, "everything but my composure."

Late Arrival

FLIGHT ATTENDANT NICOLE PERSSON noticed that the elderly gentleman remained asleep while he was wheeled aboard the New York–bound flight from Miami.

During the trip, his wife would frequently adjust his oxygen tank. When the meals were served, the wife took hers but told Nicole, "My husband is tired and doesn't want anything to eat." Later, after the dinner trays were collected and the lights were dimmed, Nicole noticed that the sleeping gentleman hadn't moved at all.

When the plane arrived at the gate, passengers pushed to get off. Meanwhile, Nicole made her way to the elderly couple and said, "The wheelchair is waiting in the jetway just as you had ordered." Then she asked the woman, "Would you like some help with his oxygen?"

"Oh no, that won't be necessary," replied the woman. "My husband died in Miami, and I am bringing him back home to New York to bury him tomorrow."

"There are two classes
of travel—first class,
and with children."

—ROBERT BENCHLEY

Polite Flight

ON A NONSTOP FLIGHT from Seattle to Salt Lake City, a first-class passenger suffered a heart attack. Because the 727 was close to its destination and the passenger was stabilized on board, Delta Air Lines captain John Burke decided to continue to Salt Lake City International Airport rather than make an emergency landing. With excellent medical facilities there, the passenger would be in good hands.

Captain Burke radioed the tower and explained the emergency and the need for an ambulance. Because time was of the essence, the Salt Lake City tower gave the captain priority landing. As the plane made its final approach, the captain announced over the PA: "Please do not leave your seats when we arrive at the gate. We have an ill passenger on board who needs medical treatment immediately. An emergency medical team will need the aisle clear when they board the plane. I will make another announcement after the passenger has been taken off the plane. Then you may get up and gather your bags. Thank you for your cooperation."

Everything went as planned at the gate: the medical team rushed on board, the passenger was removed to an ambulance, and they were able to get him to the hospital. Meanwhile, the passengers on the 727 acted like perfect schoolchildren and remained seated quietly.

And they remained that way long after the heart attack victim had been carried off the plane. That's because in all the commotion, the captain forgot about the 145 people seated behind him. For several minutes, he gathered his materials in the cockpit. When he turned around to leave, he saw 145 pairs of eyes all looking forward and all patiently waiting for him to announce they were allowed to go.

Back on the PA, the captain announced, "You've been a most courteous and polite group of passengers. Thank you for your total cooperation. You are a class act, and now class is *dismissed!*"

Stowaway Serpent

A BOY SCOUT TROOP returning home from a great week in the Michigan woods boarded a DC-8 flight from Detroit to

Newark. Without mentioning to the crew what he had in his carry-on duffel bag, one boy brought a green snake he had found during the camping expedition. As far as he was concerned, his new pet, Oscar, would be perfectly content to sleep in the overhead compartment.

Sometime during the long hours in the duffel bag, the snake slipped out. It wasn't too difficult to squeeze through the little tear in the fabric, especially for an inquisitive snake. The Boy Scout didn't realize until he got home that the reptile was missing from his duffel bag.

After several agonizing hours, he finally confessed, "Mom, I was going to bring home a snake for a pet even though you hate them. But something really bad happened on the plane. It got away. I don't know where he is, but he wasn't in my bag when I unpacked."

Shocked at the thought of a loose snake on the plane, the Boy Scout's mom called the airlines with the bad news: There might be a loose snake slithering around.

Evidently, Oscar the snake had spent several hours freely roaming the plane. The phone call came a little too late.

While boarding the next flight, an extremely startled woman found the reptile dangling from an overhead bin. Although no Boy Scouts were on board to wrestle the snake into a plastic garbage bag, one brave flight attendant caught the dangling stowaway. "I have four boys," said the flight attendant, "so I've had to deal with snakes for years. I just never got paid for doing it before."

Puke 'Em!

THE US AIRWAYS FLIGHT from Charlotte to Newark was extremely bumpy the entire way as the 737 wormed its way through one thunderstorm after another. In the cabin, passengers were turning green from airsickness.

And then it happened. It's what all flight attendants fear—the upchuck chain reaction.

The first to throw up was an eight-year-old boy. When some of his vomit landed in the lap of his ten-year-old sister, she upchucked in the aisle. Seeing and smelling the vomit, the man across the aisle tossed his cookies. The businessman in front of him, sickened by the stench, lost it, too.

Meanwhile, the mother of the two children, who was sitting by the window, was trying to stand to help clean up the kids, when she slipped and fell in the vomit after the plane lurched during the turbulence. Her dress was now caked with vomit.

Flight attendants quickly escorted the mother and children to the lavatory and gave her bottles of club soda to wash their clothes.

"It was the worst flight of my life," said Diana, a flight attendant with ten years' experience. "I had some Vicks VapoRub, so I put some under my nostrils to block out the smell and keep myself from puking. Then I tried to get the vomit up as quickly as possible before others started puking. I frantically told the passengers around the kids to stick the Vicks up their noses or else they risked throwing up too.

"Whenever I think about that flight, I still get nauseated."

Night-Night

BEING A NAVAL RESERVE SQUAD PILOT and a Delta Air Lines pilot simultaneously kept Ralph extremely busy. When he wasn't flying, he was being a wild and crazy bachelor, which also kept him extremely busy.

One weekend, Ralph was dog-tired on his way home to New Orleans from his reserve unit in Jacksonville, Florida. He caught a connecting flight in Atlanta and promptly fell asleep. When the plane landed in Louis Armstrong New Orleans International Airport, Ralph continued sleeping—even when the cleaning crew came on making noise all around him.

Later the plane took off and landed again while Ralph slept. When he woke up in Phoenix he was shocked and yelled to the flight attendants, "How come nobody woke me up?"

One of them told him they had tried in vain to awaken him. "Ralph, we know what a reputation you've got as a ladies' man, so we decided to take turns and sleep with you all the way across the country."

The Little Squirt

KATE PATRICK, sixteen, wanted to finish her homework on the flight back to Chicago after visiting her grandparents in San Diego over spring break.

She diligently tackled her vocabulary for Spanish class. Her typical routine was to review the words in the book, write them in her notebook, and then repeat them several times in her head. She also said them aloud at home, but on the plane she decided to whisper them so she wouldn't disturb the gentleman next to her.

Several minutes into her studies, she heard an obnoxious, wheezing, snorting sound. Her seatmate, with his head back on the headrest, was snoring so loud she couldn't hear herself whispering in Spanish.

Desperate for silence, Kate reached into her backpack and pulled out a dolphin-shaped squirt gun that she had bought at Sea World in San Diego. She aimed and pulled the trigger . . . squirting water into the gaping mouth of the snorer.

Grunting and snorting, he bolted upright not knowing what had taken place. *Eso es tanto major*, she said to herself. She went back to her studies without looking at him again. *That's so much better.*

" *How was my flight?*
Well, aeronautically it was
a great success.
Socially it left quite a bit
to be desired. "

—NOEL COWARD

Show Me the Money

ABOUT TWO-THIRDS OF THE WAY through the Midway Airlines flight to Orlando, a male business traveler woke up and started beating on the male passenger next to him.

Two flight attendants broke up the skirmish. "What's going on?" demanded the onboard leader.

"I had my wallet in my sports-coat pocket. It had nine hundred dollars in it," the aggressor explained. Pointing to his seatmate, he claimed, "This guy took it while I was asleep."

The accused denied the charge and threatened legal action against him and the airline if anyone pursued the matter. The flight attendant moved the accuser to another seat, but she didn't let the matter stop there.

Security met the two men at the gate when the plane landed at Orlando International Airport. After searching the accused passenger, the wallet with the $900 was found on him just as the "sleeper" had predicted.

Good Morning to You, Too

A UNITED AIR LINES 777 was flying from Chicago to Heathrow Airport in London. The all-night international flight required the cabin crew to be available to serve more than 300 people for approximately eight hours.

Shortly after takeoff, the lights were dimmed in the cabin and soon many of the passengers fell asleep. About ninety minutes from Heathrow, the lights were turned on as the flight attendants passed out warm, damp towels so the passengers could freshen up before breakfast.

Awakening from a deep sleep in business class, a middle-aged male passenger who obviously wasn't a morning person bellowed, "Who turned on the fucking lights?"

His loud swearing caught the attention of a flight attendant who was serving breakfast. In an overly sweet and cheery voice, she whispered to him, "Those aren't the fucking lights, sir. Those are the fucking breakfast lights."

It's a Small World

FLYING WITH YOUNG CHILDREN can be a real challenge for parents, other passengers, and the flight crew. Ian Hays knew he would have to be patient as well as prepared the first time he took his four-year-old son, Timmy, on a flight.

When father and son boarded the plane, Captain Terry Kelly showed Timmy the cockpit with all its gauges and instruments, and then a flight attendant gave him a pair of wings. Because he was so curious, he asked to see the lavatory and galley.

Soon lunch was served much to his delight. He giggled out loud and told the passenger next to him, "This is a mini meal. Look at the little plates."

The passenger next to him agreed. "Yes, it sure is. How do you like the airplane?"

"Everything is mini on the plane," he answered. "The bathroom is dinky and so is the kitchen. And look at this window! Even the driver of the airplane has a tiny room."

He looked at the tiny pillow and small blanket the man across the aisle was using and Timmy snickered again. "I want to work in this little place," Timmy announced to everyone sitting around him. "This plane fits me just right."

And the Winner Is . . .

AS THE CROWDED AIRLINER was about to take off, a spoiled five-year-old boy picked that moment to throw a wild temper tantrum that shattered the peace in the cabin. No matter what his frustrated, embarrassed mother did to try to calm him down, the boy continued to scream furiously and kick the seats around him.

From the rear of the plane, a distinguished gray-haired man in the uniform of an Air Force general marched up the aisle to the bratty kid and flustered mother. The courtly, soft-spoken general leaned down and, motioning toward his chest, whispered something into the boy's ear.

Instantly, the boy calmed down, gently took his mother's hand, and quietly fastened his seat belt. All the other passengers burst into spontaneous applause. As the general slowly made his way back to his seat, one of the flight attendants touched his sleeve.

"Excuse me, General," she asked quietly, "but could I ask you what magic words you used on that little boy? I could probably use them in the future one day."

The old man smiled serenely and confided, "I showed him my pilot's wings, service stars, and battle ribbons. Then I told him, 'My medals entitle me to throw one passenger out the plane door on any flight I choose, but only once a year. I haven't picked this year's winner yet.'"

Cooking His Own Goose

FLIGHT ATTENDANTS ARE TRAINED to be polite, but sometimes it can be a test of their endurance.

Jayne Trammel was collecting the meal trays one evening in first class when she asked a nicely attired gentleman, "Are you done with your dinner, sir?"

The man smirked and stated, "Fowl is *done*. People are *finished*."

It had been a long night, and Jayne's patience had been tried too many times that day. She reached over to pick up his tray and without blinking an eye said, "Are you *done* with your dinner, Turkey?"

Shocked, the man handed his tray to her. Then a big smile broke out across his face and he apologized for his comment. "That's okay," Jayne replied. "We fly turkeys all the time."

Real First Class

DRESSED IN TIGHT GIRDLES, straight skirts, high heels, and pillbox hats, flight attendants in the 1960s donned clothes not necessarily designed for comfort while working in the galleys and serving passengers. The outfits also included white gloves, which were worn before takeoffs and landings.

Corinthia, one of the first black flight attendants flying out of Atlanta in 1965, was serving dinner on an Eastern Airlines flight to Charlotte, North Carolina. The meal service was uneventful until a bigoted white woman refused to accept the dinner tray that Corinthia had offered. The woman haughtily informed Corinthia, "I will only be served by white hands."

People sitting in the surrounding rows gasped and watched the scene in stunned amazement. Everyone wondered how the black flight attendant would handle the situation. In the aisle, a white flight attendant whispered she would serve the woman, but Corinthia gently rejected the offer. Instead, she walked calmly back to the galley, put on her white gloves, and served the meal to the woman.

"Served by white hands, as you requested," Corinthia said sweetly.

As Corinthia walked away with head held high, everyone watched to see what the woman would do. She didn't acknowledge Corinthia in any way. She kept her head down and ate her dinner in silence. Later, as the passengers deplaned in Charlotte, a white passenger stopped and said to the captain, "Your black flight attendant has more class than anyone on this plane."

Airsick

"CAPTAIN HEATON, you need to come back to coach," the flight attendant said. "We've got a major problem with a man who just woke up. He's trying to open his window, and he's extremely agitated."

Recognizing the alarm in the flight attendant's voice, Captain Heaton told his first officer to take over as he rose from his seat. He donned his hat hoping to look more official in full uniform.

As he entered the cabin, he saw passengers standing in the aisle looking worriedly at the troubled man. A flight attendant sat next to him, trying to calm him.

"What kind of a plane is this if you can't even open the darn window?" the man yelled at the captain.

Drawing from his knowledge of aerodynamics and of the 757 he flew, the captain gently explained why the windows didn't open on any jumbo jets. Finally the man relaxed and accepted the lengthy explanation. As the pilot walked back toward the cockpit, the man called out, "The last plane I flew in was a Cessna 150. At least in those planes you can open the window and get some air."

It is now possible for a flight attendant to get a pilot pregnant.

—RICHARD FERRIS,
United Air Lines CEO

No Tipping Allowed

WHEN A RUSSIAN SYMPHONY ORCHESTRA and ballet troupe chartered an American-owned airplane to travel throughout the United States, they knew it would be costly, so the orchestra and the troupe met before the flight to discuss ways in which they could keep expenses to a minimum. To help defray costs, they decided on a number of things . . . all of which were surprising to their American flight attendants.

First of all, they surreptitiously carried on their own vodka, a practice frowned upon by the Federal Aviation Administration and the airlines. Of course, the group didn't ask for authorization to bring the bottles on board. The old adage "It is better to ask for forgiveness than permission" was their mantra. But they did have permission to carry on all of their musical instruments. So tucked securely in saxophone and cello cases were full vodka bottles wrapped in towels and ready for consumption.

After the plane took off, the musicians opened their instrument cases and pulled out their bottles. Music floated through the cabin as two of the violinists played songs during the cocktail hour. One of the cellists offered a drink to a flight attendant, saying, "Swig; take swig." Using her best sign language, she tried to communicate, "No, I cannot swig on duty!"

Then dinner was served. Everyone gobbled his or her food ravenously. They even ate the garnishes on their trays much to the surprise of the flight attendants, who are used to passengers complaining about the food. Then very politely, the group stood and took their meal trays to the galley. This act alone caused a huge turmoil in the aisles as the flight attendants tried to get everyone to stay seated. The flight attendants finally reconciled they would have to allow the Russians to show their appreciation their own way. "These people are better at clearing the table after dinner than my own kids," commented a flight attendant to the orchestra conductor.

Double Nookie

ON AN INTERNATIONAL FLIGHT to Amsterdam aboard an A-320 Airbus only four passengers sat in first class. One was a striking blonde who looked like she stepped out of a James Bond movie. The four were friendly and introduced themselves to each other.

They all had one thing in common—they liked champagne. Before the plane took off, they had consumed four bottles of the bubbly stuff. That fact should have alerted the cabin crew that trouble was brewing, but it didn't. Neither did the blonde's comment when asked what she would like for dinner. "I'm not going to eat," she told the flight attendant. "I'm going to drink instead."

Once the lights were dimmed the blonde turned amorous and helped induct her seatmate into the Mile-High Club. About an hour later, the blonde and another first-class passenger were entangled in some serious nookie.

When the flight attendant saw what was happening, she asked them to stop. But they paid her no attention. So in exasperation, the flight attendant threw a blanket over them, bringing a disappointing groan from the only first-class passenger who was still celibate on the flight yet hoping he would be next.

Just then the onboard leader stepped into the first-class cabin and demanded to know from the flight attendant why two passengers were thrashing around under a blanket. After hearing what had transpired, the onboard leader told the flight attendant, "Well, keep that woman away from the rest of the passengers or we'll be the first Airbus to have an entire cabin full of Mile-High members."

Hammer Help

DURING A FEROCIOUS RAINSTORM at Boston's Logan International Airport, the planeload of passengers was delayed for an hour. The pilot got on the PA and said the plane was remaining on the ground because of mechanical difficulties, not because of the weather. He said there was a problem with the emergency lights. Because it was too dangerous to take off with this lighting problem, they would have to wait for service.

Another hour passed. Finally, a mechanic walked under the wing, took out his hammer, and brutally whacked the plane five times. A moment later, the captain announced to the passengers, "We have been cleared to leave the gate now. Our emergency lights have been fixed. Sit back and enjoy the flight."

"Geez," said a passenger who had watched the mechanic, "I hope he didn't have to use his hammer to fix anything in the cockpit."

Don't Sass

JERI, A FLIGHT ATTENDANT for United Air Lines, breezed through the cabin of the 777 glancing quickly at the 300 passengers on board. The preflight safety announcement had been given, reminding everyone to stow all carry-on materials and turn off all electronic equipment. Jeri spied a businessman in first class with a cellular phone attached to his ear. Using her professional, courteous voice, she said, "Sir, you need to turn the phone off now. The captain just made the announcement there is to be no talking on cellular phones while we taxi."

Evidently, he was not in the habit of taking orders from anyone. He looked at her and replied in a condescending manner, "Can't you see? I'm not *talking* on the phone. I'm only *listening* to my voice mail."

"If you sass me again, I will take that phone away from you," Jeri said, pointing her finger in his face. "Do you hear me, young man?"

She made an impression on him. After the flight, he apologized, telling her, "You reminded me of my mama pointing her finger at me when I was growing up and telling me not to sass her."

Toupee or Not Toupee

AFTER BEING SQUASHED in the middle seat on a long flight from Philadelphia to Phoenix, Shirley decided she needed to stretch her legs and use the lavatory. The businessman next to her on the aisle seat had been intimidating the entire flight. He hadn't said hello or made any effort to be polite. Shirley hesitated to ask him to let her out of the row. Struggling to move her food tray and place books and other paraphernalia on her seat, she finally managed to stand. The displeased-looking seatmate still refused to make eye contact with Shirley. She realized he wanted her to beg him to let her out. By now, nature was calling, and Shirley felt she had to hurry to get to the lavatory.

In a polite tone, Shirley asked, "Excuse me. I am so sorry to ask you to move your legs, but I need to get out. May I please squeeze by you?"

Still, the middle-aged man did not acknowledge her. Instead, he tried to shift his legs, making it necessary for Shirley to climb over the man's bent knees. *What a jerk,* she thought.

Suddenly, the airplane hit a rough pocket of turbulence. As Shirley tried to steady herself so she wouldn't fall into the man's lap, she grabbed for the back of the seat. Somehow she missed the seat back and grabbed a hold of his hair. When she balanced herself and could stand again, Shirley looked at her hand. To her shock, she was holding the man's toupee in her tightly clutched hand. Shirley screamed at the horror of the sight.

Then in a polite tone, Shirley apologized. "I am truly sorry. Here's your head, I mean your hair, back." She tried patting the toupee onto his head, but it was on backward.

He glared at her as he straightened out his hairpiece. Then with a stone face, he tried to ignore the snickering of the passengers around him.

> *I absentmindedly poured my salad dressing into my coffee and doused my salad with nondairy creamer. . . .A kindly regional auditor sitting next to me drew the mistake to my attention. I had been consuming my meal without noticing the difference.*
>
> —CALVIN TRILLIN

Tale of the Tape

BEING A TYPICAL MALE, Paul Feyereisen loved duct tape so
much, he would experiment with it most every Saturday. In
one such test, he determined it would hold up well against a
100-mile-an-hour wind.

But Paul was not happy to see duct tape wrapped around
the right wing of the Nigeria Airways plane that he had just
boarded. Looking out at the stuff he loved, he shuddered to
think what it was holding in place. He also knew it would not
hold well at speeds over 100 miles an hour. The material he
loved to use seemed so inadequate wrapped around an airplane wing.

Should I get off the plane? he wondered. *Maybe fate is trying
to tell me something. Maybe I should listen to it. On the other
hand, there's that important business meeting I need to attend,
which means staying on this airplane. I'll have to tough it out.*

As the plane taxied down the runway, the tape rose up a
bit from the wing, revealing a giant hole underneath. Paul
could see that the hole was about two feet in diameter, large
enough to cause some serious problems should the tape come

off. The right wing was now an aerodynamic piece of equipment that was close to failing. He sat transfixed by the window, nervously watching the duct tape rise higher as it tore during the flight. Fortunately, the flight was a short one, so when the plane landed, the tape was still wrapped around the wing, although it was in shreds.

Said Paul to his business associates: "I have a newfound respect for duct tape. I'm going to call my stockbroker and buy stock in this stuff."

Hole-y Smokes

As a Southwest Airlines jet was flying over Arizona on a clear day, the copilot provided his passengers with a running commentary about landmarks over the PA.

"Coming up on the right, you can see Meteor Crater, which is a major tourist attraction in northern Arizona. It was formed when a lump of nickel and iron, roughly 150 feet in diameter and weighing 300,000 tons, struck the earth at about 40,000 miles an hour, scattering white-hot debris for miles in every direction. The hole measures nearly a mile across and is 570 feet deep."

From the cabin, a passenger was heard to exclaim, "Wow! It just missed the highway!"

Cheat Seat

SHORTLY AFTER TAKEOFF of a cross-country night flight on United Air Lines, a husband and wife in first class became embroiled in a bitter quarrel.

The wife ended the argument by turning her back to him and going to sleep. Seeing a fetching blonde across the aisle from him, the man struck up a conversation with her. Within minutes he moved into the seat next to her and began buying her drinks. Before long, he and the blonde were kissing and fondling each other.

What about his wife? She slept through it all.

Oh No, Snow!

PASSENGER BARBARA PRELLBERG tried to get to Chicago from Montana one snowy Christmas. Her flight stopped in South Dakota as it "puddle-jumped" across the northern states. When the snow continued to accumulate, air traffic control ordered the plane to turn back to Montana because Chicago's O'Hare International Airport was stacked up and would probably close due to weather.

The news was broken to the planeload of passengers by an apologetic flight attendant who said, "Travel by air when you have time to spare."

Any More Complaints?

EN ROUTE TO CHICAGO, a commuter plane stopped at Quad City International Airport in Moline, Illinois, where a few passengers disembarked. As the plane started taxiing on the runway, the flight attendant notified the pilot that one of the passengers had just awakened and realized he had missed his stop. So the pilot decided to save time by letting the man exit from the rear stairs. Ground transportation met the man and drove him back to the terminal.

The rest of the passengers did not know what was happening. All they saw was the copilot escorting a passenger out the back end of the plane, where the man collected his luggage and got into a car that had met him on the tarmac.

As the copilot closed the rear door to the plane, he entered the cabin and told the rest of the passengers, "If there are any more complaints about the food, see me!" He brushed off his hands and marched to the cockpit.

Bend Me, Shape Me

DURING A STORMY FLIGHT aboard a Boeing 737, an off-duty flight attendant was deadheading back to her home base. She sat next to a man who was white-knuckling it while he looked out the window. The aircraft's wing was bending and being twisted into shapes he had never seen before.

In order to reassure the gentleman, the flight attendant said, "Sir, I work for this airline and fly this kind of plane all the time. There is nothing for you to worry about. The pilot has everything under control. Try to sit back, relax, and undo your fingers from the armrests."

"I really appreciate your effort to make me feel better," he responded with a sick look in his eye. "But I am a Boeing engineer, and we didn't design this aircraft to do what it's doing now."

Mistaken Identity

ANN AND DICK DECIDED TO CELEBRATE their fifth anniversary by taking a bike trip in Vermont to see the fall foliage. Because they had booked their flight late in the season, they weren't able to get seats together on the first leg of the trip. When they were finally airborne, Ann wrote Dick a note:

> *Dear Seat 26C,*
>
> *I find you very attractive. Are you available to join me tonight in Vermont for a very special evening? You'll never forget it. XO.*
>
> *Wanting you, Seat 7B.*

She handed the note to a flight attendant who promptly delivered it to the man in seat 26C. A few minutes later, the attendant returned with a glass of wine, compliments of seat 26C.

After Ann finished her wine, she walked back to seat 26C only to find it wasn't Dick. He was in seat 29C.

Flushed with embarrassment, Ann approached the man sitting in the seat she had thought her husband occupied. The man looked up at her questioningly and held up the note. She shook her head and said, "I am really, really sorry, sir. I wrote that note, but it was intended for my husband over there." She pointed toward Dick.

"Wow, lucky guy," the man in seat 26C said as he handed her the note. "I bet he's gonna love reading this!"

Afternoon Delight

ONE DAY IN 1993, Love was in the air . . . while fun was on the ground.

An amorous couple in Scotland had decided to hire a pilot and his Cessna 150 for an afternoon flight over the countryside. What the pilot didn't discover until long after the plane was airborne was that the couple really wanted an afternoon delight at exactly 5,280 feet above sea level. As the plane reached the mile-high altitude, the couple in the back locked in a passionate embrace. Despite the cramped quarters, they began stripping off each other's clothes and then making love—rather loudly.

With all the couple's passionate groaning, grunting, and giggling coming from behind him, the pilot decided to let Edinburgh air traffic controllers eavesdrop on the high-flying nooner. He pushed the transmit button and left it in the on position. That way, the controllers could stay tuned in to the turn-on.

"Sounds like a hot time," a controller told the pilot. "Be careful you don't catch fire up there."

Cute Little Bugger

THIS IS A NOTE that an eight-year-old passenger wrote to the pilot during a flight from London to New York:

> *Dear Captain,*
>
> *My name is Nicola. I'm eight years old. This is my first flight and I'm not scared. I like to watch the clouds go by. My mum says the crew is nice. I think your plane is good. Thanks for a nice flight. Please don't bugger up the landing.*

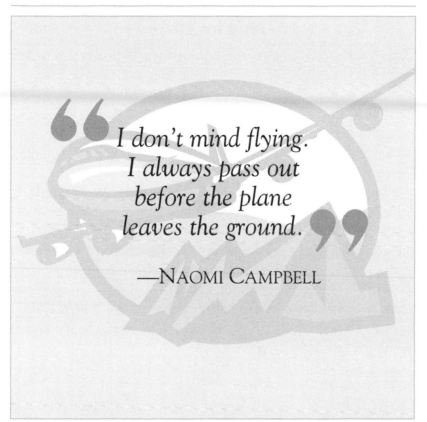

"I don't mind flying.
I always pass out
before the plane
leaves the ground."

—NAOMI CAMPBELL

No Shaggin'

ONE COUPLE on a South African Airways flight were in such heat that they couldn't resist making love right in their seats in business class. They stripped from the waist down, and started moaning and groaning in front of the shocked passengers around them. Trying not to watch at first, the other passengers couldn't help but get titillated and began to glance at the grunting, grinding couple.

After the couple ignored the flight attendant's repeated admonitions, she informed the captain of the monkey business going on in business class. "I'll handle it," he reassured her.

Moments later, the captain got on the PA and announced to the entire cabin, "This plane is not a shag house. If you are shaggin', it needs to stop immediately!"

By the time he made his announcement, the couple had finished their coupling. "I could use a cigarette," the gal said to the peeved flight attendant.

Baby On Board

SANDY AND THERESA DE BARA, from Greenfield, New York, decided to treat their three-year-old daughter, Amanda, to a memorable trip to Disney World in Florida. Their second child was due in two months, and they thought it would be a special time for the three of them to share. Once the baby arrived, they knew life would be topsy-turvy.

On the morning of November 23, 1994, Theresa felt she might be experiencing labor, so she and Sandy considered canceling the vacation. She called her doctor first, complaining of "indigestion and a little pressure." But the doctor reminded her she had gone through the same symptoms with Amanda. He told her it was probably false labor.

Sandy teased his wife of ten years, "I hope you're not going to reenact the South African Airways TV commercial where a woman gives birth on the plane."

"Oh no. That won't happen. At least it had better not." She laughed.

Immediately after takeoff, Theresa was not laughing. Rather, she was doubling over in pain. This was labor, not indigestion. Sandy got the attention of flight attendant Meg Somerville as she walked along the aisle. Meg took over without hesitation, clearing a five-seat row for a "labor and delivery room." Then she announced over the PA, "We have a woman in labor. If there is a physician on board, please report to row twenty-eight."

Dr. Steven Rachlin, an internist from Old Brookville, New York, came to help. He, too, was on his way to Disney World. His ob-gyn experience was limited—he had delivered one baby thirteen years before. After introducing himself, he took a quick look at Theresa and declared, "This lady is having a baby right now!"

While flight attendants rushed to get whatever supplies might help, the pilot radioed Dulles International Airport in Washington, D.C. The control tower cleared the airplane for an emergency landing. In the meantime, Sandy stood by in a helpless state while Amanda whimpered and cried.

As the plane began its emergency descent, Theresa gave birth to a boy. But the umbilical cord was wrapped around the baby's neck, causing him to turn blue. As the baby gasped for breath, Dr. Rachlin started CPR, massaging the infant's chest.

Just then, paramedics James and Jen Midgley of Chelmsford, Massachusetts, offered to help. Jen, whose specialty was infant respiratory procedure, asked for a straw in order to clear the baby's lungs. Although the airliner carried no straws, quick-thinking attendant Denise Booth reached into her carry-on and pulled a thin straw off a juice box that she had bought at the airport. She handed the straw to Jen.

While Dr. Rachlin continued CPR, Jen carefully steered the straw down the infant's throat. Then she suctioned fluid out of his lungs. Finally, after five nerve-jangling minutes, the baby began to cry. A shoelace taken off the shoe of a passenger was used to tie off the umbilical cord.

As the infant's wailing filled the cabin, everyone on board clapped and cheered. The captain announced over the PA, "It's a boy!"

Once on the ground, Theresa was carried off the plane as the passengers gave her a standing ovation. The paramedics whisked the baby and mother to Reston Hospital Center.

An hour later, the plane resumed its flight to Orlando with free drinks for all the passengers. Before the plane landed, the pilot announced that the baby weighed four pounds, six ounces, and that mother and child were doing well.

The onboard baby, who was named Matthew Dulles after the airport where he landed, was treated for serious respiratory problems. He remained in the hospital for three weeks before he was allowed to go home.

Later, his sister Amanda told her parents, "Now I know where babies come from."

"Where?" asked her mother.

"Airplanes."

Overhead Overblow

WHILE BOARDING a Delta Air Lines flight from St. Louis to Atlanta, a woman figured she had staked out the last available space in the overhead bin in first class. She set her bag on her seat while she took off her jacket. Before she had a chance to put her bag in the bin, a businessman beat her to the spot and placed his briefcase in the overhead compartment.

The woman was so outraged that, without saying a word, she grabbed the briefcase and flung it to the floor.

"Hey, lady!" he shouted. "My laptop is in there."

"I spotted that space first. It's mine."

"Oh? Did it have the name Bitch on it?"

Hearing the commotion, two flight attendants rushed over before the man and woman came to blows over the treasured overhead real estate. When the combatants continued to argue, the flight attendants threatened to throw them off the jet.

Finally, they worked out a peaceful solution. The woman was allowed to use the space that she had claimed, while the flight attendants put the businessman's briefcase up front with the cabin crew's personal belongings.

As order was restored, the businessman pointed to the overhead bin and whispered to one of the flight attendants, "That space would've been better served if you would've stuffed her in it."

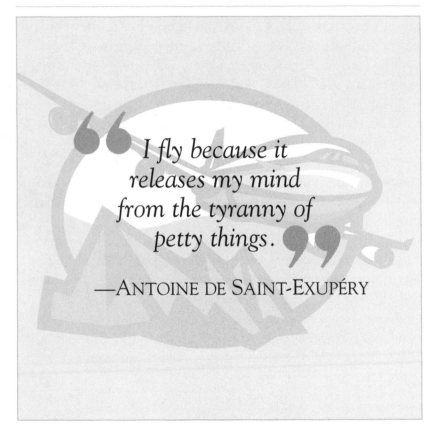

I fly because it releases my mind from the tyranny of petty things.

—ANTOINE DE SAINT-EXUPÉRY

Carrying On over Carry-ons

EVER WONDER what goes through people's minds when they decide to bring on board items that can't possibly fit in the overhead bins?

Anne, a Delta flight attendant for over twenty-five years, thought the windshield for a compact car was the largest item she'd ever seen a passenger try to carry into the cabin.

Passenger Steven Fleming looked on with bemusement when a passenger insisted on placing a set of antlers in the overhead bin. They wouldn't fit, but the passenger still refused to check them. Frantic negotiation ensued. The captain finally kept them in the cockpit.

Jim, an AirTran pilot, watched as a passenger tried to lug a 45-by-60-inch framed painting into the cabin. Jim finally convinced the gentleman to get it wrapped and checked. Yes, it arrived in Michigan in perfect condition.

Keith, another AirTran pilot, observed a man and woman holding full, large garbage bags on their laps. They adamantly refused a flight attendant's request to put the bags in the overhead compartment, so Keith was summoned to talk to them. The couple explained they had all their earthly belongings stuffed in the bags and they were afraid of letting them out of their sight. He talked them into storing the bags in the compartment.

Cheryl, a new flight attendant, knew she should expect the unexpected. A kayak paddle wasn't surprising and neither was a large couch cushion the passenger was returning to a furniture store. But her biggest shock was seeing a man carrying two legs for his friend who followed in a wheelchair.

Among other items that passengers have tried to bring on board: a car muffler, a four-foot-tall urn, a stuffed coyote, a potted hemp plant, a nude and anatomically correct mannequin, a stuffed swordfish, a garbage bag of snow, and bundled kindling.

Love Them Vittles

ON A US AIRWAYS FLIGHT, a passenger from the Deep South who had never flown before was asked by a flight attendant if he would like the chicken or the pasta entrée for dinner. He thought for a minute and answered, "I guess I'll try the second one, the possum."

Squirmy Situation

TWO SNAKES SLITHERED OUT of their containers during an Alaska Airlines flight, causing squeamish passengers to sit with their feet on the seat.

The woman who brought them on board with her was in violation of airline policy. She had not notified the airline of her traveling companions. Even if she would have notified them, the only policy on snakes is no snakes in the cabin.

When the snakes, which the woman claimed were harmless, escaped, she was considerate enough to inform the crew, who launched a frantic search in the cabin for the missing reptiles. Passengers shrieked and stood on their seats when a snake was sighted.

The captain considered making an emergency landing in Juneau, but before he could carry out that contingency, the snakes were captured, herded into secure bags, and then stowed in a closet.

The cabin crew tried to use a touch of humor to ease passengers who were stressed by the snake escapes. For dinner, passengers were told, "Tonight we have chicken, steak, or a third choice that rhymes with *goodness' sakes*."

A Real Oinker

MARIA TIROTTA ANDREWS brought her pet Vietnamese pot-bellied pig, Charlotte, on board a US Airways flight after the airline had agreed to let her 13-pound pig fly with her. She had stated she needed Charlotte as her companion for "therapeutic" purposes.

Charlotte was considered by the airlines to be a service animal because it provided relief to Andrews's heart condition. The Federal Aviation Administration allows service animals to accompany disabled persons. In this case, Charlotte was allowed to sit in first class, free of charge . . . even though, when Maria and her pet arrived at the gate, Charlotte actually weighed 300 pounds, not 13.

A number of customers on the October 17, 2000, flight from Philadelphia to Seattle filed complaints with the airline stating the pig was disruptive and unruly. During the six-hour flight, passengers reported, Charlotte ran around first class, bumped the cockpit door, and wouldn't budge from the galley. Finally, a creative passenger threw food into the aisle to get her to move. "My pig did not run around anywhere," Andrews stated.

FAA spokesman Jim Peters defended the airline by saying, "US Airways and its personnel acted in a reasonable and thoughtful manner, based on a legitimate request to transport a qualified individual with a disability and her service animal." All guidelines were followed, so no charges were made against US Airways.

What Kind of Fool Am I

"GUS" GUSTAFSON WAS NOT an experienced international traveler, although he flew a few trips within the continental United States each year. Long flights over the ocean scared him and he tried to keep that embarrassing information to himself.

When the vice president of the company suggested they take an overseas trip together, Gus sighed. He spent several sleepless nights leading up to the actual trip, but once on board, he started to settle down a bit and control his anxieties.

As the jumbo jet started its takeoff roll down the runway, the vice president looked at his watch and announced smugly, "Wheels up in thirty-two seconds. Not bad." Gus was impressed even though he had no other numbers to compare it to.

In Europe, they each went their separate ways on business. Five days later, Gus caught a flight back to the States. As luck would have it, he was seated next to a gorgeous lady in business class. Gus sipped champagne while waiting for the plane to fill. He was smiling at his good fortune of having such a lovely lady next to him for the long flight.

They made polite conversation while the plane taxied to its runway. Then, as the plane revved its engines for takeoff, Gus decided to impress the woman. He removed his watch and started to time the takeoff, emulating what he had seen his VP do earlier in the week. The plane started to roll. When the wheels didn't go up at thirty-two seconds, he started becoming concerned. At forty seconds, he broke out in a cold sweat. At forty-five seconds, he was panicked. Finally, at forty-nine seconds, the plane lifted off the ground as sweat dripped profusely off his forehead. He let out a huge sigh, which gained the attention of his seatmate.

She was so underwhelmed by his panic attack, she put the *Times* of London in front of her and never spoke the rest of the transatlantic flight.

Voters Win

THE 1999 WEATHER FIASCO in Detroit where hundreds of passengers were left on planes stranded on the runway for eight hours caused most of the airlines to review their policies. Giving passengers advance notice of delays and cancellations has since become a priority.

A United Air Lines Boeing 777 left the gate as scheduled at Chicago's O'Hare International Airport at 1:23 P.M. for Washington's Dulles International Airport. But the takeoff was delayed because of a snowstorm on the East Coast. No specific time was given for the plane to leave because the

Federal Aviation Administration was waiting out the storm. At 6:55 P.M.—five and a half hours after the plane left the gate—the 777 returned to the gate to refuel. Once refueled, the plane went back out to the runway. Salads and small sandwiches were given to first-class passengers. The rest of the passengers devoured all the peanuts and snacks.

The plane went back to the gate at 9:04 P.M. to let a member of the flight crew off. (Regulations for all commercial airlines restrict the number of hours a crew member may work on a flight. If the employee reaches that maximum level in a twenty-four-hour period, he or she may not fly. Crew members must be given specific number of hours off between flights for rest.) Passengers were given the opportunity to vote on taking off or waiting for more food to arrive. Overwhelmingly, they voted to leave.

Majority ruled, and the plane taxied again to the runway. At 9:53 P.M.—exactly eight and a half hours late—the plane took off.

Raphael Minsky, a passenger, said, "If we really thought we were going to get a hot meal, we might have waited. But everybody said, 'Let's get this plane off the ground and go.'"

"It's like being in a pressure cooker to be an air traffic controller."

—DON BIGGS,
Pressure Cooker

Grossed Out

WHAT'S THE GROSSEST EXPERIENCE you've ever had on a commercial flight?

"The guy next to me took off his shoes and stunk up the whole cabin with his smelly feet. What was even worse, he clipped his toenails and left the clippings all over the floor. It was disgusting."

—JOE WARSHAWSKY

"We had just finished what passed for an airplane meal when my seatmate began flossing her teeth. Bits and pieces of food were flying all over the place."

—NANCY CUSHION

"This is so gross I get queasy just talking about it. This old codger across the aisle had a cup and he kept coughing up phlegm into it. He'd gag and then spit into this clear plastic cup, so you could see all the green junk. I almost heaved my guts out. How's that for a gross-out?"

—JIM GALLO

"I saw a kid pick his nose with his finger and then examine the loogie as if it was a thing of beauty."

—MARY HARTWELL

"The person next to me was a big, fat slob who pulled out cotton swabs and was cleaning out his ears. Then you know what he did? He actually began playing with his earwax, you know, like making little shapes out of it with his thumb and index finger. I just buried my head in my book."

—ROB RIXSON

"This woman in her twenties had short dark hair and was wearing a black blouse. She kept shaking and scratching her hair and all these dandruff flakes landed on her blouse. She got Scotch tape out of her briefcase and began deflaking herself."

—HANK OSBURG

Out to Pasture

ONCE, ON A SHORT FLIGHT from Los Angeles to San Francisco, a young woman named Jenny was seated next to actor Eddie Albert. This was during the time when he was the star of the TV sitcom *Green Acres*.

She felt so sophisticated sitting next to a real celebrity that she resisted the desire to ask him a million questions. In fact, she didn't bother him at all . . . until turbulence caused her to puke in the airsick bag.

Moments later, the flight attendant came over to Jenny and told her that her seat assignment had been changed. She escorted Jenny to the rear of the plane, far away from the *Green Acres* star.

Said a chagrined Jenny to the flight attendant, "Gee, I feel as if I've been sent out to pasture."

Brush-Off Lines

OBNOXIOUS SEATMATES often need more than a subtle hint that nobody wants to talk to them. Here are some measures that passengers have successfully used in the past:

"Tell them you are in insurance and need to meet your quota. Nothing I've found is as effective."

—DAN BURKE

"Look out the window and excitedly ask, 'Do you think we'll see any UFOs today?' Guaranteed, seatmates won't even look at you the rest of the flight."

—MIKE BORSE

"Go to the IRS Web site and download their emblem. Lay it on the top of your business pages. A cover letter downloaded from the CIA's site works well, too."

—CHRIS NEEDHAM

"If the plane isn't full, sit in a center seat and lean over so your head is in the airsickness bag. If somebody still tries to sit down, lean over and cough like you're coughing up a fur ball. People will avoid you."

—TOM FOLENTA

"In extreme cases, put in earplugs, tie on a blindfold, and pretend to sleep."

—RON HRANAC

In the Lavatory

Seeing Is Believing

WHEN A SEEING-EYE DOG TRAVELS with its master, the dog is seated on the cabin floor next to the owner. In general, seeing-eye dogs have a wonderful reputation, as they guide their masters and wait patiently next to them on the flights. If there are any problems with them, it's usually not the dogs' fault.

On a flight from Miami to San Juan, an eighty-pound German shepherd quietly sat in first class next to its master. Halfway through the flight, the gentleman decided to use the lavatory. Usually, the dog will wait at the seat, but this traveler wanted his dog to accompany him. The flight attendant escorted the two of them to the lavatory at the front of the plane.

Because it was a tight squeeze in the lavatory for the man and his best friend, the door did not completely close.

Noticing the door was slightly ajar, a flight attendant tried to shut it but wound up accidentally smashing the dog's tail.

Suddenly, the door flung open. The yelping dog ran to the middle of the aisle in first class and shook frantically as passengers and food were covered with yellow droplets.

It took a few moments before everyone realized what had happened. Then they were grossed out. When the dog's tail was caught in the door, the shepherd bumped into its owner, who was standing over the toilet relieving himself. The man was thrown off balance and accidentally urinated on his dog. The wet German shepherd then burst out of the lavatory and sprayed several of the unfortunate passengers when it shook its coat.

"I felt so bad for everyone," recalled the offending flight attendant. "I was just trying to help."

Lavatory Lust

ON A FLIGHT TO NEW ORLEANS to celebrate the first Mardi Gras of the new millennium, a guy and a gal who had never met before they were seated next to each other decided to let the good times roll. After some winking and whispering, they sneaked into the lavatory, where they got to know each other in more intimate detail. About the time when the weather outside became as wild as the action inside the lavatory, the pilot turned on the seat-belt sign.

The flight attendant knocked on the door to inform the occupant and was startled to hear a man and a woman giggling inside. She ordered them to get out and back to their seats, but they ignored her. After rapping on the door several more times, the flight attendant gave up and sat down until the turbulence—the turbulence outside, not inside—had subsided.

All the commotion ruined the couple's amorous rendezvous. Eventually, the two sheepishly exited the lavatory. They apologized to the flight attendant, who met them in the aisle and gave them a harsh lecture. She even took their names to be filed with the Federal Aviation Administration.

"That guy sure wasn't worth it," the woman whispered to the flight attendant. "It'll be a while before I try the Mile-High Club again."

The Tooth Fairy

"MISS, MISS!" the female passenger whispered as she tapped flight attendant Lane Hall's arm. Beckoning with her index finger, she said, "Come see what I've found."

Lane's curiosity was aroused by the woman's whispering voice and strange smirk. Lane walked to the rear of the 727 to the lavatory, where, floating in a sink full of water, there was a pair of false teeth.

After thanking the now-giggling passenger, Lane removed the false teeth from the sink, wiped them, and placed them on a serving tray. She put a white linen napkin over the tray and left the galley. She walked from the front of the plane to the rear before spotting the sunken mouth of an elderly lady. Discreetly, Lane lifted the linen cloth and asked, "Are these yours?"

The embarrassed lady nodded and took her teeth.

When the 727 landed in Dallas/Fort Worth International Airport an hour later, the elderly woman gave Lane a big hug and said, "Who would have ever thought at my age I'd still believe in the tooth fairy? But I sure do—and I've met her today. Thank you, Tooth Fairy."

There are only two reasons why anyone would want to sit in the back of an airplane. Either you have diarrhea or you want to meet people who do.

—HENRY KISSINGER

Giving an Erotic Earful

A NEWLYWED COUPLE who had been pawing and kissing in the waiting area at Chicago's Midway Airport still couldn't keep their hands off each other after they boarded a Kiwi flight for their honeymoon in West Palm Beach, Florida.

During the flight, the happy lovebirds slipped into the rear lavatory together and within minutes were making purrs of passion loud enough to be heard by the flight attendants and passengers in the back. Several of them actually stood around the door and received an erotic earful.

By the time the flushed and sweaty couple had finished and returned to their seats, word had spread throughout the cabin of their sexploits. Shortly before arriving at Palm Beach International, one of the flight attendants informed the captain that there were two new members of the Mile-High Club on board.

As the plane arrived at the gate, the pilot got on the PA and said, "Good afternoon, ladies and gentlemen, and welcome to Palm Beach International. I'd also like to welcome our two newlywed passengers into the ranks of the Mile-High Club." The entire cabin broke into cheers and wolf whistles.

The couple grinned in bewilderment at first, not knowing exactly why everyone was applauding them. When one of the flight attendants told them what the Mile-High Club was, all the color drained from the young bride's face. Meanwhile, her new husband broke into an ear-to-ear grin.

John's John

SOME PEOPLE are just plain cheap.

A male passenger who was freshening up in the lavatory of a DC-9 accidentally dropped his false teeth into the flushing toilet. First Officer John was summoned by a flight attendant to the lavatory to solve the problem. John tried to explain to the passenger, "I can fly the plane, but I don't know much about the john. Sorry! We weren't taught anything about plumbing in flight training."

The passenger accepted the explanation. Although nothing could be done during the flight, John assured the passenger that once they landed in St. Louis, the cleaning crew would assist in locating the choppers.

After the plane arrived, the cleaning crew came onboard and tried to retrieve the false teeth but were unable to do so from inside the plane. So they went outside and drained the toilet tank. The workers found the false teeth floating in the disgusting slime of the blue toilet solution and returned them to the passenger.

"Thanks, guys, I appreciate what you had to go through to get these for me," he said. "I'll drop these into some of that fizzy stuff tonight, and they'll be good as new tomorrow."

Now Arriving: Flight 255—and a Baby

JOELLA SISON, a twenty-five-year-old housewife from Valdosta, Georgia, didn't think too much of the fact she was gaining weight. She blamed her overeating on stress, since her husband, Richard, an Air Force pilot, was serving in the Persian Gulf War.

While Richard was away on duty in 1991, Joella took her two children, ages one and two and a half, to stay with her mother in California. When Richard completed his tour of duty, he returned to California. Little did they know that their family was about to get larger.

The day the Sisons were supposed to fly back to Georgia, Joella felt sick. She complained to her mother, "I'm getting these sharp pains across my stomach. They come and go."

"It sounds like you're in labor," her mom quipped.

It may have been a joke, but Joella didn't laugh. She knew she wasn't pregnant. Other than the weight gain, she had shown no signs of pregnancy. All she knew was that she felt miserable and couldn't get herself in a comfortable position. Nevertheless, she wanted to return home so her family could get on with their lives.

Despite the pains, she boarded Atlanta-bound Delta Air Lines Flight 255 with her husband and two children. After the plane took off, the pains became intense. Joella decided to use the rest room, where she hoped to regain her strength and collect herself. But the pains didn't cease. Instead, her water broke and Joella suddenly realized her mother's words were so true. She was in labor.

Minutes later, Joella delivered a baby boy in the lavatory. She opened the door and called out to the flight attendant, "Help me! I just had a baby!"

The flight attendant, startled by the yelling, came running and looked into the small lavatory. After reassuring Joella that everything would be all right, the flight attendant made an announcement over the PA asking for medical assistance. Two doctors and a nurse came forward to help.

Meanwhile, Richard and the two children had no idea why Joella had not returned to her seat. After she had been gone for nearly fifteen minutes, he headed to the lavatory to see if she was all right.

"What's going on?" he asked the flight attendant when he saw the crowd of doctors and nurses around the lavatory.

"Oh, a passenger has just given birth to a baby on board," the flight attendant answered excitedly.

Richard peeked over her shoulder and gasped, "That's my wife!"

Cradling the baby in her arms, Joella gazed at him and introduced him to his new son. "Say hello to the boy we didn't know we were having."

Reeling in unimaginable shock, Richard couldn't believe his own eyes. "This is the biggest shock of my life!" he declared for all to hear. Actually, it was pretty amazing for everyone else on the plane, too.

Because the nearest city was Albuquerque, New Mexico, the plane made an unscheduled landing there, where six-pound newborn James Paul and his mother, accompanied by the rest of the family, were taken to the hospital. The flight then continued on to its destination. Due to minor medical problems caused by the rapid delivery, James was kept in the hospital for ten days.

When he was ready to go home, Delta flew the entire Sison family home first class. The proud father announced, "I'm really happy to be a dad again, even if I wasn't expecting this one. Maybe he'll grow up to be a flyer like his dad. He's got an early start."

Cat-astrophe

As a DELTA AIR LINES flight attendant for twenty-eight years, Anne thought she'd seen almost everything. One night serving first-class passengers, she and another flight attendant were confronted with a medical problem.

One of the female passengers started hyperventilating. Her traveling companion rushed her into the lavatory telling her to calm down and relax. Unfortunately, the words were not reassuring. While the victim gagged for air, she lost control of herself and urinated all over the lavatory. Her companion looked helplessly at the flight attendants, who stood in the doorway aghast.

Anne stood aside as her coworker administered mouth-to-mouth resuscitation on the stricken passenger. Her efforts failed, and somewhere over Utah, the passenger died in the flight attendant's arms. The passenger was a furry little pet cat.

> *There is an art to flying. The knack lies in learning how to throw yourself at the ground and miss.*
>
> —DOUGLAS ADAMS,
> *The Hitchhiker's Guide to the Galaxy*

In the Galley

What's in a Name?

NORMA HILLIARD, a veteran Delta Air Lines flight attendant, was preparing beverages in the galley on a full TriStar L-1011 heading to Los Angeles. With 280 passengers on board, she knew there would be many beverage cups to fill, so she was busy trying to get the setup cart ready.

Just then, a middle-aged woman appeared in the galley with her eyes fixed on the plastic cups with the Delta logo on them. "What do you do with the used cups after you collect them?" she asked Norma.

The flight attendant replied, "After they are used by the passengers, we throw them away, of course."

"Well," the woman hesitantly asked, "would you mind saving them for me?"

Norma looked at the woman quizzically and thought, *This lady is crazy!* But instead of sounding disrespectful, she inquired, "Why do you want a planeload of dirty plastic ware?"

"My daughter is getting married next month, and we could use them for the reception," replied the passenger. "I'll just wash them first."

"But they have 'Delta' written on them," Norma pointed out, beginning to feel this would be a long flight.

"Yes," the woman said, smiling. "That's great, because Delta is our last name."

"I'd love to give them to you, but I can't. I have to throw them out. I hope you understand, ma'am, but it's our company's policy to discard all used items because of health reasons. I guess you'll just have to find plastic cups for the wedding elsewhere."

After they landed, the flight attendants did their usual check of the plane before leaving. That is when Norma noticed the trash bag containing the used, discarded plastic glasses was missing from the galley.

Pee Ode

ST. PATRICK'S DAY, 2001, was a day many passengers on a Boston-to-Pittsburgh flight will never forget.

Dressed in a stylish green shirt, coat, and pants, a young man boarded the plane singing "Oh Danny Boy." He had obviously been celebrating the day by drinking green beer. But he did not appear to be too intoxicated . . . just extremely happy. He found his seat along with his buddies, who were equally in a celebratory mood.

After the plane reached cruising altitude and the seat-belt sign went off, "Danny Boy" decided he needed to relieve himself. The aisles were clear except for the area outside the galley, where the flight attendants were preparing to serve dinner.

The young man was drunker than he appeared because he mistook the galley for the lavatory. Without noticing that he was standing in the galley, he unzipped his green pants and sprayed the meal-tray carriers while the flight attendants froze in horror and disgust. With the cheerful smile of a leprechaun, he then returned to his seat, whistling "Oh Danny Boy."

All the food was thrown out. The passengers were told that meals wouldn't be served on the flight because of an "unexpected problem with the food."

Hearing the announcement, one of the passengers who had witnessed the revolting sight shouted, "What a pisser!"

Dead Weight

NEARING THE END of an Eastern Airlines flight from New York to San Juan, Puerto Rico, flight attendant Lane Hallwood went to a special closet next to the galley in the front of the plane where the jackets and coats of the first-class passengers were hanging. She began gathering the garments and returning them to their owners. She liked this part of her routine because it meant that the long flight in the L-1011 was almost over. This particular trip was, thankfully, extremely uneventful. Or so she thought.

After passing out almost all the jackets and coats, she reached into the closet and noticed that a garment bag had fallen in a crumpled heap to the closet floor. Hoping the items inside were not wrinkled, Lane bent over and tried to rehang it. But the bag was bulky and extremely heavy. She didn't remember ever hanging it up. *A passenger must have put it in there when I wasn't looking,* she thought. Just then, the captain announced that the flight attendants needed to take their seats and buckle up for the landing.

Lane left the garment bag on the floor until the plane stopped at the gate. Then she quickly went to the closet but couldn't lift up the garment bag because of its weight. Curious, she unzipped the bag to readjust the contents. Seconds later, she let out a scream. Inside, the shocked flight attendant discovered the frail, dead body of an elderly woman!

Hearing the commotion, a middle-aged man who had placed the garment bag in the closet came forward to explain. The woman was his eighty-three-year-old mother, who had passed away earlier that day. She had been ill for several months and had made her son promise that, upon her death, he would take her back to her homeland for burial. He was just trying to be a dutiful son, he told the still-stunned flight crew. Authorities escorted him—and the body of his mother—off the plane, where they buried the man under a mound of questions and paperwork.

When Push Comes to Shove

AS THE A320 AIRBUS TAXIED to a complete stop at the gate, the United Air Lines flight attendant announced, "Thank you for flying with us today. Please remain in your seats until the airplane has come to a full stop at the gate. Then everyone can jump up, push, shove, and try to be the first one off the airplane."

Freebie

DURING THE PREFLIGHT safety announcement, a flight attendant told the passengers: "Your seat cushions can be used as a flotation device. In the event of an emergency water landing, please paddle to shore and take them with our compliments."

Cruisin'

SHORTLY AFTER A SOUTHWEST AIRLINES FLIGHT took off, the pilot announced to the cabin: "We've reached our cruising altitude now and I'm turning off the seat-belt sign. I'm switching to autopilot, too, so I can come back there and visit with all of you for the rest of the flight."

*" You define a good flight
by negatives: You didn't get
hijacked, you didn't crash,
you didn't throw up,
you weren't late, and you
weren't nauseated
by the food. "*

—PAUL THEROUX

She Sprays for You

SOME DAYS it seems nothing goes right.

Ready for her first day as a Delta Air Lines flight attendant trainee, Cathy Wenske stood smiling as the passengers boarded the plane. She knew it was important to make a good first impression, especially when greeting the passengers. Her cheerful smile beamed on her twenty-year-old face.

But underneath her smile, she was a bundle of nerves, because she so wanted everyone to like her. She masked her nervousness by trying to exude confidence. Of course, everyone knew she was new on the job and had no experience thanks to the large badge with "Trainee" written on it. She tried hard to overcome the badge's declaration of her lack of experience.

Before takeoff, cabin service began in first class, where she offered beverages to her passengers. As she carefully opened her first can of soda, her thumb slipped, and the can fell onto the floor. It was partially open, so a light spray of the beverage flew up on the lady who had requested it. As Cathy bent down to pick up the can, she, too, was sprayed. Then the can rolled down the aisle spraying the first-class passengers.

Apologizing profusely, she offered vouchers for dry cleaning to all those who'd been sprayed. The passengers who had been doused the most accepted vouchers.

One woman passenger wearing shorts tried to make light of the situation. "When I go in the lavatory to wash my legs of the soda, I might as well shave my legs. I didn't have time this morning before I left home."

Eating on the Run

AFTER MEAL SERVICE had been delayed because of turbulence, there wasn't much time to eat, but the cabin crew decided to feed the passengers anyway. To ease the somber mood of the passengers, who had endured the rough weather, the onboard leader made this announcement on the PA:

"We are flinging your meals tonight, so get ready to catch them as we run up and down the aisle."

What a Gas

THERE WERE TWO THINGS about Wendy, a flight attendant from Alabama, that made people like her the moment they met her. First, she talked in a folksy southern drawl that charmed most every passenger. Second, she loved to party off duty.

On one particular flight, Wendy was hung over from drinking too many Bloody Marys the previous night. Nevertheless, she was a professional and performed her duties flawlessly while looking forward to the end of the flight.

Unfortunately, because of bad weather at its final destination, Atlanta, the jetliner was forced to circle over the Tennessee-Georgia border. After nearly an hour of circling in the stormy skies, the pilot announced, "We're getting low on fuel, so we're being diverted to Nashville to refuel."

Passengers groaned—and so did Wendy, whose stomach was twisting and turning. All she could think about was getting on the ground and away from all the irritations of the job: the bumpy ride, the noise of the jet engines, and the pungent smells of the lavatory and discarded food.

While she was leaning in the galley located in the center of the plane, a man rushed up to her. Excited with worry, he whined, "I know we're gonna crash! We don't have enough fuel! We'll never make it to the airport!"

Wishing the pilot had never informed the passengers of their low-fuel situation, Wendy looked at the passenger and said in her sweet drawl, "Honey, don't you worry: Now y'all go take your seat 'cause I have enough gas in my stomach to get us to Nashville and beyond."

Autopilot

AT MEALTIME DURING A FLIGHT, one of the flight attendants will often bring the captain a pillow to put on his lap so he can balance his meal on it. The cockpit doesn't have fold-down trays like those in the cabin. Because it's a long way to bend over and eat, especially if the pilot doesn't want to spill food on his lap, it's helpful to have the pillow.

One evening, a woman who was nervous about flying was seated behind the curtain in coach. She watched the flight attendant carry a tray and a pillow into the cockpit. Making an assumption without all the facts, the passenger stood up and yelled, "Oh no! I just saw in the cockpit—one's gonna eat and one's gonna sleep! Who's gonna fly the airplane?"

When the flight attendant returned from the cockpit, she told the frightened woman not to worry because, "they put the plane on autopilot."

Time Is on Our Side

WHILE THE PLANE WAS BEING BOARDED at Detroit Metro Airport, a sweet lady asked Mitchell, the Northwest Airlines flight attendant, "Young man, I don't understand how this flight can arrive in Chicago at eight-thirty-three A.M. If we leave on time here, it will be eight-twenty A.M. That's only thirteen minutes to go all the way to Chicago."

Mitchell patiently tried to explain, "Ma'am, Michigan is one hour ahead of Illinois. We're in the eastern time zone and Chicago is in the central."

The sweet lady persisted. "I still don't know how it only takes thirteen minutes."

With a kind smile on his face, Mitchell answered, "This airplane goes really, really fast."

The sweet lady understood that and took her seat.

No Age Limit

DURING A PREFLIGHT CABIN ANNOUNCEMENT, the flight attendant told the passengers: "Should the cabin lose pressure, oxygen masks will drop from the overhead area. Please place the mask over your own mouth and nose before assisting children or other adults acting like children."

Finders Keepers

FROM A FLIGHT ATTENDANT'S CABIN ANNOUNCEMENT: "As you exit the plane, make sure to gather all of your belongings. Anything left behind will be distributed evenly among the flight attendants. Please do not leave children or spouses."

Cleaning Crew

FROM A FLIGHT ATTENDANT'S CABIN ANNOUNCEMENT after the plane arrived at the gate: "Last one off the plane must clean it."

Painfully Aware

AFTER AN EXTREMELY HARD LANDING, a flight attendant announced, "Ladies and gentlemen, as you are all painfully aware, we have just landed in Anchorage. From all of us who served you, we'd like to thank you for flying with us today. Please be extremely careful as you open the overhead compartments. You may be injured by falling luggage that shifted during our crash lan—I mean, our touchdown."

Short and Sweet

FROM A FLIGHT ATTENDANT ON A COMMUTER FLIGHT: "Okay, folks, listen up. This is a short flight, so I'm only going to make this announcement once. . . ."

Telling It Like It Is

BEFORE LANDING, a brutally honest flight attendant told the passengers: "We are about to land. Please make sure your seat is in the upright and most uncomfortable position."

Smoking Can Be Hazardous to Your Health

FROM A FLIGHT ATTENDANT before takeoff shortly after the Federal Aviation Adminstration banned all smoking on U.S. planes: "This is a nonsmoking flight. If you must smoke, please ring your flight attendant call-button and one of us will escort you out to the wing. Any passenger caught smoking in the lavatory during our flight will be asked to leave the plane immediately."

Blockheads

FROM A FLIGHT ATTENDANT to passengers who were still stowing their bags in the overhead compartments as the plane began to push back from the gate: "Folks, you have to sit down. When you're all standing up and blocking the aisle, the pilot can't see to back up."

Rubbing It In

AFTER A HARD LANDING in Amarillo, Texas, the American Airlines flight attendant rubbed it in to the pilot by making this cabin announcement: "Ladies and gentlemen, please remain in your seats until Captain Crash has brought what's left of the plane to a screeching halt up against the gate. Once the tire smoke has cleared and the warning bells are silenced, we'll open the door. Hopefully, you will be able to pick your way through the wreckage to the terminal."

Jest Tube

AS THE US AIRWAYS PLANE TAXIED TOWARD THE GATE, the flight attendant told the passengers: "We'd like to thank you folks for flying with us today. We know you have several choices in carriers to this destination, so we are happy you chose to fly with us. The next time you get the insane urge to go blasting through the skies in a pressurized metal tube, we hope you'll do it with us here at US Airways."

You haven't seen a tree until you've seen its shadow from the sky.

—AMELIA EARHART

Stewed

PAN AM'S DISTRUST OF ITS FLIGHT ATTENDANTS proved costly for the airline.

In the early 1980s, Pan Am bigwigs were convinced that flight attendants were stealing thirty-five-cent miniature liquor bottles on flights. So airline security personnel rigged up a unique device. It was a clock secured to the liquor cabinet in the galley that would record the number of times the cabinet was opened. The security people figured the alleged thefts would then be recorded, so punishment could be delivered. No one told the flight attendants because it was hoped they would be caught with their hands in the liquor cabinet.

While airborne one day, a flight attendant heard a strange ticking sound coming from the liquor cabinet. Thinking it was a bomb planted on the plane, she notified the captain. Immediately, the plane was rerouted to the nearest airport. Passengers were evacuated by the emergency exits upon landing. Security personnel stormed the plane only to find the timing device ticking in the liquor cabinet.

The undercover investigation came to a screeching halt when they realized they couldn't determine when any alleged unauthorized happy hour began without costing the airline any more money. The unscheduled landing had cost Pan Am $15,000. Management's attempt to uncork the culprits was foiled. Besides, there was never any proof the stews were getting stewed for free anyway.

Bite This

WHEN AIRLINES MERGE, customer service often nose-dives.

In February 1987 on a Continental Airlines flight from Denver to Miami, passengers complained about the dinner. The meal consisted of a cold roast beef sandwich, potato chips, and an apple. As the complaining continued to sizzle, a flight attendant began to boil and soon exploded like a pressure cooker. Over the PA, the onboard leader confessed he was "embarrassed" about the "substandard" food.

"This is a Frontier airplane," he explained. "Frontier Airlines was recently bought by People's Express, which was bought by Texas Air, which also bought Continental.

Continental Airlines' catering service is handling the flight, and their trays don't fit into our ovens."

The passengers were then invited to send the comment cards from the in-flight magazine to Texas Air executives. Within a few minutes, the flight attendant discovered that none of the magazines had comment cards left. It appeared the previous passengers on this plane had a similar problem. Seething in frustration, the onboard leader gave out the office address of Texas Air chairman Frank Lorenzo. Said the unnerved flight attendant, "He's responsible." So the passengers wrote letters chewing out the chairman. Their battle cry was "Bite the big one!"

Leaving on a Jet Plane

FROM A SOUTHWEST AIRLINES FLIGHT ATTENDANT giving the preflight cabin announcement: "There may be fifty ways to leave your lover, but there are only four ways out of this plane."

Good Business

FROM A FLIGHT ATTENDANT'S CABIN ANNOUNCEMENT after landing: "Thank you for flying Delta Express. We hope you enjoyed giving us the business as much as we enjoyed taking you for a ride."

Above All

AFTER A PARTICULARLY ROUGH LANDING during a thunderstorm at Memphis International Airport, a flight attendant on a Northwest Airlines flight announced to the passengers: "Please take care when opening the overhead compartments because, after a landing like that, sure as hell everything has shifted."

Choices, Choices

FROM A SOUTHWEST AIRLINES FLIGHT ATTENDANT during her preflight cabin announcement: "To operate your seat belt, insert the metal tab into the buckle and pull tight. It works just like every other seat belt, and if you don't know how to operate one, you probably shouldn't be out in public unsupervised. In the event of a sudden loss of cabin pressure, oxygen masks will descend from the ceiling. Stop screaming, grab the mask, and pull it over your face. If you have a small child traveling with you, secure your mask before assisting with theirs. If you are traveling with two small children, decide now which one you love more."

What Would Mr. Greenjeans Think?

A FLIGHT ATTENDANT'S CABIN ANNOUNCEMENT on a less-than-perfect landing: "We ask you to please remain seated as Captain Kangaroo bounces us to the terminal."

Flight Attendant Lingo

HERE ARE SOME TERMS USED BY FLIGHT ATTENDANTS among themselves when they're talking about passengers:

Ball-gown clown: A female passenger dressed for an evening at the Savoy; often seen carrying her stilettos due to her swollen feet.

Newlyweds and nearly deads: Typical passengers on a cruise-destination flight usually going to Florida or California.

Upgrades: Those upgraded passengers who immediately adopt a superior attitude.

Squishes: Passengers who are loath to accept or ask for a much-needed seat belt extension.

Obstacles: Passengers who wait until they see a meal trolley coming before they get up and go to the lavatory.

White knuckles: Bug-eyed, hyperventilating passengers who are fearful while the plane is still on the ground, get even more scared when the plane takes off, and freak out when the plane hits air turbulence.

Thumpers: Passengers who take great pleasure in bumping, kicking, and shaking the seats in front of them.

Thumpees: Passengers sitting in front of thumpers who often seek revenge by abruptly reclining their seats, preferably when the thumpers have hot beverages on their trays.

Dreamer: A male passenger deluded enough to believe that a flight attendant will invite him to join the Mile-High Club.

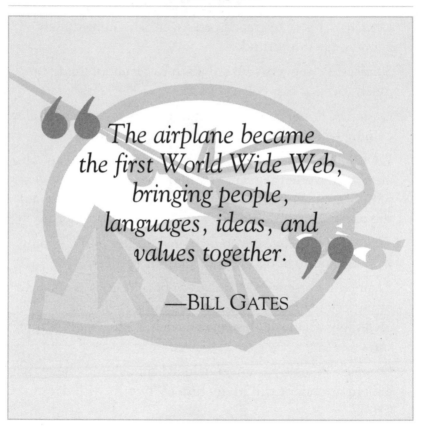

*The airplane became
the first World Wide Web,
bringing people,
languages, ideas, and
values together.*

—BILL GATES

In the Control Tower

What's Missing?

AIR TRAFFIC CONTROLLERS have a stressful job. They work in two areas: terminal control and en route control. The job has been compared to playing a three-dimensional chess game, yet the responsibility they have is no board game. Sometimes the only thing funny that happens to them all day is listening to pilots on the radio.

Fred, a controller, was working in New York at John F. Kennedy International Airport on a typical day—busy. A 747 called him saying, "This is United at the gate. We're ready to push back."

"Push back is approved, United," Fred directed. "Taxi to runway three-right."

A few moments went by and the United captain came back on the radio. "Aah, Ground Control, we'd like to change that direction and hold."

"Is there a problem?" asked Fred.

"Well, sir, we haven't boarded any passengers. Oversight. Sorry to bother you."

Roadkill

TOWER: TWA 702, cleared for takeoff. Contact Departure on 124.7.

TWA 702: Tower, TWA 702 switching to Departure. . . . By the way, after we lifted off, we saw some kind of dead animal on the far end of the runway.

TOWER: Continental 635, cleared for takeoff. Contact Departure 124.7. Did you copy the report from TWA?

CONTINENTAL 635: Tower, Continental 635 did copy TWA, and we've already notified our caterers.

Say What?

O'HARE APPROACH CONTROL: United 329 Heavy, your traffic is a Fokker, one o'clock, three miles, eastbound.

UNITED 329: Approach, I've always wanted to say this. . . . I've got the Fokker in sight.

Sounds Familiar

WHILE TAXIING AT NEW YORK'S LAGUARDIA AIRPORT, the crew of a US Airways flight to Fort Lauderdale made a wrong turn and came nose to nose with a United 727. The irate female ground controller verbally lashed out at the US Airways crew, screaming, "US Air 2771, where are you going? I told you to turn right on 'Charlie' taxiway. You turned right on 'Delta.' Stop right there. I know it's difficult to tell the difference between Cs and Ds, but get it right!"

Continuing her lashing to the embarrassed crew, she was now shouting hysterically. "You messed everything up. It'll take forever to sort this out. You stay right there and don't move until I tell you to! You can expect progressive taxi instructions in about half an hour, and I want you to go exactly where I tell you, when I tell you, and how I tell you! You got that, US Airways 2771?"

The ground control frequency went silent after the verbal bashing of US Airways Flight 2771. No one wanted to engage the irate ground controller in her current state. Tension was running high in every cockpit at LaGuardia. Eventually, after the controller finished her heated admonishment of the US Airways crew, an unknown pilot who had been listening in broke the silence and asked, "Wasn't I married to you once?"

Retirement Planning

AN AIR TRAFFIC CONTROLLER who was uncertain what a pilot was planning to do radioed, "Please state your intentions."

Before giving a professional answer, the pilot replied, "I intend to retire to a small farm in Georgia and raise peaches."

It's Only Money

THE AIR TRAFFIC CONTROLLER WAS WORKING a busy pattern and told the 727 on downwind to make a three-sixty (do a complete circle, usually to provide spacing between aircraft). The pilot of the 727 complained, "Do you know it costs us two thousand dollars to make a three-sixty in this airplane?"

Without missing a beat, the control tower replied, "Roger, give me four thousand dollars' worth!"

Hearing Aid

WHEN THE PILOT OF A JETLINER that had just taken off from Chicago's O'Hare International Airport failed to acknowledge a controller's command, the controller told the captain, "You're going to have to use your microphone, sir. I can't hear you when you just nod your head."

Do You Know the Way to San Jose?

A DC-10 HAD AN EXCEEDINGLY LONG ROLL-OUT after landing because his approach speed was just a little too fast. As the plane sped down the runway trying to stop, the San Jose control tower said, "American 751 heavy, turn right at the end if able. If not able, take the Guadelupe exit off Highway 101 and make a right at the light to return to the airport."

The pilot laughed at the tower at having so little faith in his stopping ability. He sang back on the radio, "Yes, I know the way to San Jose."

Car Talk

IT WAS A REALLY NICE DAY, right about dusk, and a Piper Malibu was being vectored into a long line of jetliners in order to land at Kansas City International Airport.

KC APPROACH: Malibu Three-Two Charlie, you're following a 727, one o'clock and three miles.

THREE-TWO CHARLIE: We've got him. We'll follow him.

KC APPROACH: Delta 105, your traffic to follow is a Malibu, eleven o'clock and three miles. Do you have that traffic?

DELTA 105 (long pause and then in a thick southern drawl): Well . . . I've got something down there. Can't quite tell if it's a Malibu or a Chevelle, though.

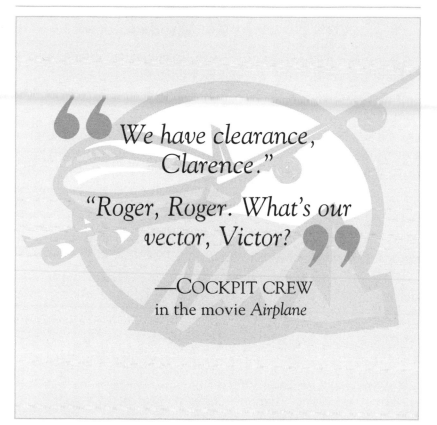

"We have clearance, Clarence."

"Roger, Roger. What's our vector, Victor?

—COCKPIT CREW
in the movie *Airplane*

It's Faster in the Windy City

WHEN A JETLINER FROM ATLANTA was nearing Chicago's O'Hare International Airport, the pilot told the tower in a southern drawl, "We have slowed down to two hundred twenty [knots]."

"Pick it back up to two hundred fifty [knots]," the air traffic controller ordered. "This ain't Atlanta and them ain't grits on the ground."

Bear in Sight

THE AIR TRAFFIC CONTROLLER said to the aircraft that just landed, "Bear right, next intersection."

Answering back, the pilot said, "Roger, we have him in sight. I think he's a grizzly."

Good Intentions

THE AIR TRAFFIC CONTROLLER SAID TO THE PLANE, "Cessna G-ABCD, what are your intentions?"

The student pilot flying the Cessna answered, "To get my commercial pilot's license and instrument rating."

Shaking his head in the control tower, the controller replied, "I meant in the next five minutes, not next five years."

Space Saver

THE PILOT OF A JETLINER complained to the tower at Chicago's O'Hare International Airport that he wanted more room between his plane and the one behind him.

The controller, who obviously had an acerbic wit, replied, "If you want more room, sir, push your seat back."

Fueling a Misunderstanding

THE PILOT OF THE CESSNA said relatively calmly, "Jones Tower, Cessna N7033CC, student pilot. I am out of fuel."

The air traffic controller thought the kid sounded too calm to believe. Maybe he was in shock. So gently the tower responded, "Roger, Cessna N7033CC. Reduce airspeed to best glide. Do you have the airfield in sight?"

The student answered, "Uh . . . Tower, I am on the south ramp. I just want to know where the fuel truck is."

Keep It Quiet

THE PILOT OF UNITED 402 requested a clearance from 25,000 feet to cruise at an altitude of 31,000 feet: "United 402 requesting climb to flight level 310."

The air traffic controller quickly responded, saying, "United 402, maintain flight level 250 for noise abatement."

The pilot was surprised that noise was any concern way up at his altitude and asked the air traffic controller, "What do you mean maintain 250 'for noise abatement'?"

The controller replied, "If you climb and hit the traffic at 270, there will be a big noise."

Do-It-Yourself Kit

THE PILOT OF A CHEROKEE 180 was instructed by the tower during his taxi to hold short of the active runway while a big DC-8 landed. When the jet landed, the pilot of the DC-8 radioed the Cherokee pilot, "What a cute little plane. Did you make it yourself?"

The Cherokee pilot answered, "I sure did. I made it out of DC-8 parts. Another bad landing like the one you guys just made, and I'll have me some spare parts."

The Three Bears

THE AIR CANADA EMPLOYEE FLYING CLUB was extremely proud the day its four-seater Cessna 172, newly painted in the airline's colors, rolled out of the hangar for the first time. It was tiny in comparison to the other planes in the Toronto maintenance base.

Meanwhile, the pilot of an Allegheny Air Lines jet radioed the tower and said, "Toronto Ground, this is Allegheny 357. I'd like taxi clearance."

The tower answered back, "Roger, Allegheny. Hold short. You have an Air Canada L-1011, an Air Canada DC-8, and an Air Canada Cessna 172 passing in front of you."

Allegheny answered, "How cute: Papa Bear, Mama Bear, and Baby Bear."

Nude Awakening

AFTER MISSING THEIR FLIGHT HOME to Turkey to attend the funeral of a dear friend, three men, including one who knew how to fly, rented a King Air turboprop in Berlin, Germany, in 1994. The pilot filed a flight plan to head directly to Izmir,

Turkey. While flying over the Czech Republic, the pilot learned that the Turkey ATC had denied his flight plan. "What do we do now?" the pilot asked the Czech controller.

Strangely, the Czech controller told the pilot to use the code for "hijack in progress." This would allow them priority status so they could follow the flight plan they had requested moments earlier. The pilot thought it was an unusual instruction, but he followed directions even though he knew that crying wolf could be dangerous. He would soon discover how dangerous.

All across his flight path—Slovakia, Hungary, Romania, and Bulgaria—air traffic controllers' screens lit up with a warning of the hijacking in progress. The King Air zoomed its way toward Turkey, but it was denied landing at Izmir. *It's strange not to be given clearance*, thought the pilot.

He went on to Lesbos, a Greek island, where he was given clearance to land. Authorities there questioned the pilot and his passengers, who assured them that no hijacking had occurred. Once they had apparently cleared up any misunderstanding, the pilot and his buddies were allowed to leave and continue on to Turkey.

When they arrived in Izmir, they were shocked at their reception. It became obvious that the misunderstanding had not been cleared up. Fire trucks, tanks, police, and armed guards all converged on the plane and its passengers. But then came an even greater surprise. The trio were completely strip-searched right there on the ramp. They were all stark naked—proving they had nothing to hide and were not hijackers.

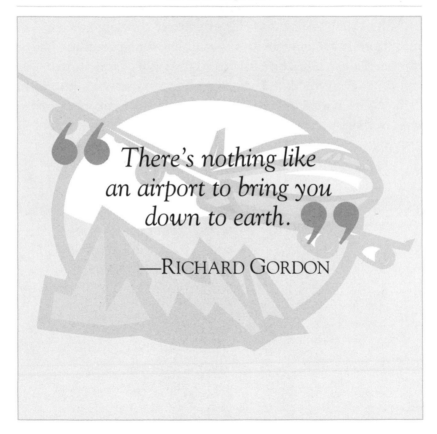

There's nothing like an airport to bring you down to earth.

—RICHARD GORDON

In the Cargo Hold

Gone to the Dogs

IN ADDITION TO HIS TWO CHILDREN and wife, Larry Murphy also had two pets to move when he was transferred. The human beings were easy to move, but moving the French poodle Puff Puff and the mixed-breed hound Snooky proved to be much more difficult. The move was from Brunswick, Georgia, to Mobile, Alabama. Larry's parents kept the dogs at their home in Brunswick until Larry was ready for them in Mobile. Weeks later, his parents crated the dogs and put them on a plane bound for Alabama.

Larry first suspected there was a problem when he arrived at Mobile Regional Airport and was told the dogs would arrive on a later flight. When the plane arrived, Larry was ushered into the airport manager's office and then told a wild tale of the tails. While the dogs were on the tarmac in

Hartsfield Atlanta International Airport waiting to be loaded onto the connecting flight to Mobile, a jet's exhaust knocked their crates off the loading cart. Both crates broke open and the two frightened dogs bolted onto the tarmac as several airport employees chased them with nets. Big jets were coming in and out of the gate area. The hound bit three people before being caught. A tow truck hit the little French poodle while on the tarmac, but she sustained only minor injuries.

When Larry finally retrieved his pets, he was amused to see the signs on each of their crates: "CAUTION: MEAN DOG. BE CAREFUL. DO NOT OPEN." Inside the crates sat two terrified, howling dogs who made it clear to the family they never wanted to fly on an airplane again.

Paws for Concern

A HOUSE CAT SINGLE-PAWEDLY cost an airline thousands of dollars in extra fuel, delayed passengers for three and a half hours, and caused others to miss their connections.

In 1990, Continental Airlines Flight 119 boarded fifty-three passengers for a relatively short, two-hour flight from Fort Lauderdale, Florida, to Houston, Texas. But just after takeoff, the pilot of the Boeing 727 noticed a light on the control panel indicating the heater to the cargo section of the plane was not working. There was no danger to the plane or the passengers, but the captain still faced a life-or-death decision

He knew in the cargo hold there was a house cat in a carrying case belonging to one of the passengers. The air in the hold was growing colder as the jet climbed higher. If the plane continued its ascent, the temperature in the hold would reach fifty degrees below zero and kill the furry fluff ball.

So, after getting clearance from the tower, the captain turned the plane around and announced to the passengers they were returning to Fort Lauderdale. "The pilot said there was a mechanical problem, and he certainly didn't tell us the problem was a feline," recalled passenger Bob Schachner. "Only after we returned to the airport did we learn why we had come back. They opened up the cargo door and pulled out the carrying case to see if the cat was still alive. It was a tuxedo cat—black and white with a white stripe—and it was fine. The owner was so relieved."

Despite the fact the interruption cost the airline thousands of dollars and was an inconvenience to the passengers, the pilot was praised for his life-saving decision. "It was just good customer care," said Ken Gordon, Continental's general manager at Fort Lauderdale. "After all, I've got a cat, too."

Lost and Found

TWICE IN 1991, missing cats created havoc for the airlines. Irving Robinowitz, a plump Himalayan cat, escaped from his carrying case while he was being placed in the cargo hold of a Continental Airlines jet at Newark International Airport. Evidently, Irving had a feline's fear of flying. His adventures on the ground at the airport had far-reaching implications because the flight was grounded for more than an hour. While airport workers frantically searched for the fleeing feline, Irving tiptoed into the employees' break room and went into hiding.

To avoid further delaying the other frustrated passengers, the cat's heartsick owners, Helen and Ralph Roselli, asked Continental to end their search and take off without their pet. Their suggestion was accepted, and the plane left without Irving.

Two hours into the flight, the pilot made an announcement, "Mr. and Mrs. Roselli, they found Irving, and we'll fly him back tomorrow." To celebrate, the flight attendants served free booze to all the passengers, who had cheered and applauded the pilot's good news.

The next day, true to its word, Continental returned the cat to West Palm Beach, Florida. The fur flew home in style—in first class.

Months earlier, a cat named Bobby had a much more harrowing experience before he was given the VIP treatment. In a rebellious mood one day, Bobby wandered away from home not heeding the calls of his owner. He somehow pranced his way to nearby Houston Intercontinental Airport (now George Bush Intercontinental Airport) and climbed into an unheated, unpressurized wheel compartment of a Pan Am jet.

Incredibly, he survived the extremely thin air and below-zero temperatures on the 1,700-mile trip to New York City. After the plane landed, mechanic Gary Hickman heard loud meowing coming from the landing gear. There he discovered the greasy, scared, but unharmed, Bobby. "I thought, 'Holy cow! How could this little guy still be alive?'" recalled

Hickman, who gave the scaredy-cat oxygen and milk. Even though he had been trapped in the wheel well, Bobby survived the ordeal.

This cool cat was turned over to feline-loving pilot Paul Scholz, who flew Bobby home while the animal sat on a bundle of blankets in the cockpit. He was personally fed poached salmon, one of his favorite dishes. What some cats won't do for a free fish dinner!

"It's a miracle Bobby survived the flight and didn't fall out when the landing gear was lowered," Scholz said.

Back in Houston, the pilot found Bobby's owner, Elaine Nolan, through the cat's rabies tag. "I think it is all so crazy," she said. "But I am so glad Bobby is home."

Bahama Mama

BECAUSE 1985 HAD BEEN A SLOW YEAR for William at work, he and his wife, Pammy, decided not to take a vacation. However, as summer grew closer, William realized they really needed to get away. Being somewhat of a romantic, he planned a surprise long weekend. "A romantic getaway was just what Pammy deserved after taking care of two children all year," William later recounted.

He surprised her by leaving a note saying, "You are my Bahama Mama. Pack a swimsuit and toothbrush and nothing else." He had worked it out for friends to watch their two children while they went to the Bahamas, so Pammy was ready to go when he arrived home from work.

He had arranged for them to hitch a ride on a charter flight full of vacationers. As the plane neared the islands, the weather turned bad in Freeport, so the plane was put in a holding pattern. That's when the flight attendant made an announcement: "We realize this plane is scheduled to go to Freeport, Bahamas, but we have an unusual request. Many people told us when they were boarding that they would rather go to Nassau. The pilot has checked with Nassau, and we may land there instead of Freeport. Please raise your hands if you would rather go to Nassau." Pam and William looked around the cabin. Everyone else had a hand up.

Then the flight attendant asked, "How many of you would like to go to Freeport?" Pammy and William were the only two hands raised.

The flight attendant approached them and said, "We'll see that you get to Freeport after we land in Nassau." William explained he had already paid for the hotel in Freeport and they absolutely had to get there.

After four hours of waiting in the Nassau airport, William and Pammy felt they would never get off the ground. Then a gate agent escorted the couple to a waiting cargo plane. William and Pammy climbed into the back with the mailbags.

As the plane taxied down the runway, it came to a stop because several goats were slowly crossing the runway and had priority clearance. When the plane finally took off, the couple decided to make the most of their slight change in plans. Snuggled closely together between the large overstuffed bags of mail on the cargo plane, William and Pammy became new members of the Mile-High Club somewhere between Nassau and Freeport.

*The scientific theory
I like most is that
the rings of Saturn
are composed
entirely of lost
airline luggage.*

—MARK RUSSELL

Roasted Goat

IN THE SPRING OF 1994, a Malaysia Airlines 747 had to return to Perth, Australia, within a short time after takeoff. The plane was bound for Kuala Lumpur with a load of 190 goats.

The animals had started roasting sooner than they should have. All alive and on the hoof, their body heat generated so much heat in the hold of the plane that it triggered a fire alarm. Fortunately, everyone survived the ordeal—but the goats eventually ended up on the plates of many Malaysians.

Extreme Cold for Dakota

HALFWAY THROUGH A FLIGHT from Washington, D.C., to San Jose, California, in June 2000, passenger Mike Bell was startled when the captain of United Air Lines Flight 231 asked to speak to him.

The pilot explained there was a problem involving Bell's beloved ten-year-old dog, a basenji named Dakota, who was on the flight in the baggage section of the plane. The problem was, said the captain, that the dog had been mistakenly placed with luggage rather than in the area specifically for animals. When the captain was notified of this error two hours into the flight, he explained the situation to Bell. It was likely that the dog could not survive in the cargo bay without heat.

"I was speechless," Bell recalled later. "My eyes were getting watery." No one knew if Dakota could survive the cold temperatures of the cargo bay. The tender-hearted captain announced to the passengers that they would be making an unscheduled stop in Denver, the nearest airport. "The wait was agonizing while I thought about how strong-willed and stubborn Dakota was," said Bell, a thirty-eight-year-old software-quality-assurance manager.

As soon as they landed, Bell and the captain ran to the tarmac and watched the baggage handlers unload the crate containing Dakota. To Bell's relief, his dog had survived the bitter cold. Bell was allowed to bring the dog on board, and as he entered the plane, cheers and applause went up from the passengers. They had not minded the "paws" in travel, since it meant saving the pooch.

Clearing the Vault

LUFTHANSA'S OPERATIONS TRAINING CLASS tried to instill the importance of giving specific written handling directions. Based on the assumption that oral communication often breaks down, the operations teacher stressed to the students they must carefully write procedures for loading the plane, handling the cargo en route, and unloading the plane. Most students paid close attention to instructions, but some did not.

If there was any special-handling paperwork accompanying the pole vault on the A320 Lufthansa flight, it didn't arrive in Barcelona for the 1992 Summer Olympics. The pole vault had been loaded in Frankfurt for Barcelona, but the ground crew did not include any specifications with it. No one had a clue how to unload it in Spain. It would not bend in order to get it through any of the doors. After several phone calls to Frankfurt, the dilemma was solved. A high loader was driven to the plane, the captain's window was opened, and the Olympic pole vault was removed through the window.

Inflatulation

THE PILOT OF A LUFTHANSA CARGO PLANE was not given any specific information regarding his load of live pigs. He did not know that their flatulence would infiltrate the cargo compartment. Nor did he know what effect the odor would have on the crew, including himself.

Nearly overcome by the odor of flatulent pigs, the captain was faced with a problem. The plane was within thirty minutes of its destination, but the foul air was so obnoxious, something needed to be done immediately. He decided to depressurize the aircraft, thus stopping the circulation of air throughout the plane.

His idea seemed to work, as the smell decreased during the last few minutes of the flight. When the unloading process began, the crew found a load of dead pigs—all asphyxiated from lack of oxygen.

What a Crock

LACK OF COMMUNICATION almost proved fatal in Stuttgart, Germany.

Two large tubular containers sat unclaimed in the Lufthansa cargo area in the airport. No written work was attached to the containers; no questions were asked; no one missed them or inquired from their destination point.

Finally, a curious employee decided to investigate and opened one of the containers. Sound asleep lay a crocodile. In the other container, his traveling companion was also resting. They were accidentally detained and contained in Stuttgart while traveling to a zoo in the Far East.

I decided there must be room for another airline when I spent two days trying to get through to People Express.

—RICHARD BRANSON,
on creating Virgin Atlantic

At Corporate Headquarters

Fear of Flying

PACIFIC AIR LINES, a small but enterprising West Coast commuter carrier, wanted an attention-grabbing campaign that would send profits soaring. Instead, PAL ran commercial aviation's most shocking promotion—one that sent the company into a tailspin.

In 1967, PAL sought the help of the irreverent comedian Stan Freberg, who moonlighted as a Los Angeles–based ad consultant. Freberg suggested PAL poke fun at the one thing all other airlines never mentioned—fear of flying. And he wasn't referring to Erica Jong's book by the same title.

Many of the carrier's executives were aghast and warned the campaign would never get off the ground with the flying public. But PAL's president, Matthew McCarthy, told Freberg to fly with the idea.

Under the comedian's direction, PAL placed full-page ads in New York and Los Angeles newspapers that read: "Hey there, you with the sweat on your palms! It's about time an airline faced up to something—most people are scared witless about flying. Deep down inside, every time that big plane lifts off that runway, you wonder if this is it, right? You want to know something, fella? So does the pilot, deep down inside."

Most pilots were outraged by this false declaration and were ready to ground Freberg. Meanwhile, PAL added some zany touches on its flights to help people laugh at their fears. Flight attendants gave passengers survival kits containing a pink rabbit's foot for good luck. They also handed out Norman Vincent Peale's book *The Power of Positive Thinking*. To top it off, fortune cookies were distributed with the message, "It could be worse. The pilot could be whistling 'The High and Mighty.'" Last, but not least, when the plane touched down, flight attendants were told to say loudly, "We made it! How about that?"

If all this wasn't enough, to give shaky airborne passengers a feeling they were still on the ground, PAL planned to draw the cabin shades and project pictures of telephone poles whizzing by. They planned to paint the outside of their 727 jets to look like old steam locomotives, complete with wheels and cowcatchers. The sounds of a locomotive would play throughout the cabin.

The initials PAL took on a new meaning—"Passengers aren't laughing." Not surprisingly, the airline industry was in an uproar. Executives from other carriers feared the promotion was scaring potential customers away from air travel in general. "Lots of people are terrified of flying, and we thought it was time somebody cleared the air," scoffed McCarthy.

The bizarre promotion definitely cleared the air—of PAL planes. Within two months, the airline was no more.

Affairs of Mate

THE UNITED AIR LINES "Fly Your Wife Free" campaign in the late 1970s, in which businessmen were encouraged to bring their wives along gratis, was deeply flawed. Only United didn't know it—until it was too late.

Many businessmen took advantage of the terrific offer. What a promotion—a free trip for their sweethearts! The campaign was a success until United took it one step too far.

Trying to be nice, the airline sent letters of appreciation to the customers who flew with their partners. The problem was that the letters were sent directly to the customers' home addresses. Soon United was inundated with angry letters from outraged wives. They claimed they had never heard about the promotion much less been invited to accompany their husbands on a free trip. They demanded to know the names of the recipients who had flown with their high-flying husbands.

United was dismayed and perplexed. It had not anticipated the infidelity nor the rage. Following its policy of protecting the privacy rights of all passengers, the airline had no official comment. The philandering husbands had to fend for themselves.

Ground Feed

FRONTIER AIRLINES and Continental Airlines took their fare wars to a Denver billboard in 1986. One of Frontier's billboards, just outside the city's airport, promised the carrier would "change this board" of its claim that it flies for less if any competitor could undercut Frontier's fares.

When a new ticket policy at Frontier left Continental with lower fares for fourteen days, Frontier failed to change its billboard. So several Continental executives promptly set up camp under the Frontier billboard. They added insult to injury by erecting a tent atop a rented bus and stringing out a thirty-foot banner. The banner declared to Frontier and everyone else: "We'll be here until you tell the truth."

Continental further antagonized its rival by offering free meals at its ticket counters to any and all Frontier passengers, pointing out Continental didn't charge extra for meals on their flights. Not satisfied yet, Continental went on to announce it was giving free sodas to Frontier pilots, saying it felt sorry for them because they had to pay fifty cents for a soda on their own flights.

Frontier sought a truce by sending some free snack boxes to the enemy camp beneath the Frontier billboard. These were the same kinds of snacks that were served on Frontier flights for an additional $3.00. But the Continental campers were not content to accept the truce. Instead, they had the contents of the snack box analyzed. They smugly announced the food inside was worth only $1.26. They bit the hand that fed them. Frontier finally conceded.

Relabel Black Label

TO IMPROVE THE QUALITY of the booze in coach class in 1980, Alvin Feldman, then president of Continental Airlines, stocked up on Chivas Regal Scotch. His next dilemma was what to pour in first class. To answer that very serious question, he sought the advice of a Beverly Hills bartender who suggested Johnny Walker Black Label.

That solution didn't fly too high with the first-class passengers. They glared with envy at the budget-minded folks in the aft sipping good old Chivas. To keep tempers from flaring, flight attendants began smuggling Chivas Regal from coach into first class.

Eventually Chivas Regal became the official hootch for both classes on Continental Airlines. After the final decision was made, a Continental spokesman said the airline had enough bottles of Black Label Scotch to last for years. But one industrious high-flying passenger suggested, "Relabel the Black Label 'Chivas Mislabel Regal.'"

> A recession is when you have to tighten your belt. A depression is when you have no belt to tighten. When you lose your trousers, you're in the airline business.

—SIR ADAM THOMSON

The Naked Truth

IN AN EFFORT TO ENCOURAGE a more diversified flying clientele, Braniff Airlines executives enlisted the assistance of an ad agency to attract more Hispanics in the United States. This decision took place in 1987, and it left people thinking they would be flying nude.

The ad, which was run on Spanish-language television and radio stations, touted Braniff's leather seats. The radio commercial told listeners to fly *en cuero*, which means "in leather." But a similar Spanish expression, *en cueros*, means "naked"—and the two phrases sound identical when spoken quickly.

Even more eye opening was the television commercial version, which invited travelers to fly *"en cuero"* and *"con tres pulgadas más,"* meaning "with three inches more." Presumably, the airline was referring to the extra legroom on their planes. However, those people who thought the voice-over said *"en cueros"* received an entirely different message.

The commercial went limp quickly. The TV ad was pulled when the other meaning was revealed. And the ad agency was red faced due to their unintentional oversight. "We were caught with our pants down," remarked a Braniff official.

Enter at Your Own Risk

NORTHWEST AIRLINES HAD A GREAT IDEA for a promotional contest in 1981. The only problem was, they had forgotten about a very dear relative of theirs—Uncle Sam.

The grand prize was almost unbelievable. It was the use of a Boeing 727 jet with pilot for a round trip to Fort Lauderdale, Florida, and three nights in a luxury hotel. The winner would be allowed to bring ninety-two of his or her closest friends and relatives.

It was a fantastic dream trip for ninety-three people. As it turned out, it was a little too fantastic.

The airline trumpeted the contest in full-page ads in Midwest newspapers, stating, "Win a jet to Florida and take ninety-two friends along. Take your relatives. Take your coworkers. Take your church group, lodge, or neighbors."

When the grand-prize winner was picked, his joy turned to concern. Once he started looking into the tax ramifications, he realized one of the people he might want to talk to first before accepting the prize was his accountant. That's because the accountant could explain what Northwest failed to mention—that the winner could lose his shirt.

The grand prize constituted taxable income. The winner of the promotion would be forced to cover the added taxable income for his friends. If the winner made use of the full value of the prize, he would add $50,000 to his taxable income for 1981. In order to offset this shocking detail, the airline said they would toss in $15,000 to help the winner pay this added tax burden. But that idea never got off the ground—because the cash gift was also taxable. The winner skipped the free jet trip and took a cash settlement instead.

Message in a Bottle

IN ORDER TO DEMONSTRATE Pan Am's superior service on the hotly competitive New York–San Juan route, the ad agency J. Walter Thompson came up with a cute idea. The premise was a picnic-style lunch to be served to the passengers.

A small bottle of Portugese Mateus wine, sliced salami, cheese, and an apple would be presented in a little plastic basket on a dainty gingham tablecloth. Newspaper ads were prepared to announce the picnic promotion, but pesky little details kept springing up like picnic-frenzied ants.

The first snafu came when airline officials read their contract after 2,000 pounds of salami arrived already sliced. Pan Am's commissary contract stipulated that all meats must be sliced by the commissary butchers.

The ad campaign was put on the back burner while the sliced salami was returned and a rush order was placed for a ton of whole salami. After the salami arrived and was sliced by the commissary, the airline realized it had another problem with its picnic promo—the baskets were in New York and the wine was in San Juan. The right hand didn't know what the left hand was doing. To make matters worse, the wine was then flown to New York while the baskets flew past them en route to San Juan. Evenually, the two items were united in the same airport.

The executives were beginning to wonder if they would ever see the ad campaign come to fruition, but the baskets were finally assembled, the ads were aired, and the flight was a sellout. Pan Am's excitement and happiness, however, was short-lived. On the maiden flight, the flight attendants had no cork screws in order to open the bottles of wine. The 180 passengers were ready to break the bottles over the flight attendants' heads.

Pan Am returned cases of Mateus wine to Portugal in exchange for screw-capped bottles. Finally, it looked as if the promotion would take off as planned. But there was to be one last downpour on their picnic: Pan Am had put on larger airplanes to San Juan. Now they were flying 747s, which held 300 passengers. The assembly and service required for that many people was deemed too much of a hassle for the flight attendants, and Pan Am ditched the campaign.

Pet Peeves

AIRLINES HAVE BEEN CHANGING their pet policies, and some passengers have devised ingenious ways of getting around the restrictions.

One woman tried to bring her cockatiel on board in her purse. Other passengers have tried to take pets along disguised as service animals, according to Robert Ashby, attorney for the U.S. Department of Transportation.

In San Rafael, California, the nonprofit Guide Dogs for the Visually Impaired has received calls from people wanting to rent harnesses so they can disguise their pets. Of course, the organization is not allowed to lend harnesses for any animals other than guide dogs. "It sheds a bad light on service animals in general," commented spokesperson Joanne Ritter.

A woman flying round trip between Washington and Chicago on American Trans Air brought her two Pekingese dogs. Each dog was given its own seat. Another passenger claimed he suffered an "allergic reaction" to the dogs. American Trans Air spokesperson Mary Cochrane said that under the law, "we were merely meeting our obligations."

In the meantime, the airlines accept monkeys that are assisting quadriplegics, as well as Great Danes, Labradors, and a wide variety of other service animals, all of which are not caged and ride free of charge.

Not According to Webster

WESTERN AIRLINES had a term for its flight engineers. The term was *GIB*, for, "guy in back." Because he was not in one of the two front seats in the cockpit, he was referred to as the guy behind the captain.

The term was strictly unofficial and was actually frowned upon by management at Western. It seems that some wise-guy pilot had been browsing through a dictionary and had made the discovery that a *gib* was a castrated tomcat.

Tough Old Bird

MAINTENANCE IS A CONTINUOUS PROCESS for planes of all sizes throughout the world. Testing the equipment ensures flight safety, which is the number one objective of the airlines. Even the windshield is tested periodically for its strength. In order to test the windshield, it is first heated and then subjected to a blast from a cannon firing a dead chicken traveling at a speed of 300 miles per hour. Because airplanes share the skies with birds and on occasion run into one or more of them, a dead chicken is used for testing purposes. The initial heating of the windshield helps its flexibility during the test. In actuality, the windshield is usually cold at high altitudes.

Because testing equipment is expensive, it is occasionally shared among the airlines. Recently a British airline borrowed a special cannon from an American airline. The maintenance expert who usually accompanied the equipment was unavailable for this scheduled testing, so the cannon arrived in England without him.

Unfortunately, the first test was disastrous. The chicken smashed the windshield, ripped through the back of the pilot's seat, and finally embedded itself in the wall directly behind the cockpit. A second test ended with the same dreadful results. Obviously, the pilot would have been seriously injured if this had taken place on a real flight.

This test was proving costly because of all the damage it was inflicting. *Something must be wrong with the test*, the British airline's maintenance engineer thought. Before breaking another windshield, he called his counterpart at the American airline that owned the cannon.

"What are we doing wrong?" the British engineer pleaded. "We're breaking windshields, ripping up seats, and putting holes in the wall. This can't go on!"

After the American engineer asked several questions, he soon figured out the solution to the dilemma. "Thaw the chicken!" he ordered.

Barf Bags

"AN AIRLINE WITHOUT BAGS is like an airplane without wings," Bill Wivchar stated. He would know because he used to order approximately 1.2 million bags each year for Trans World Airlines.

Even though the Federal Aviation Administration no longer requires barf bags to be on board, every airline continues to place one in each seat back. Many other airline amenities have been cut over the past decade, but the barf bags are still available and probably will always be. Amazingly, over 20 million bags are sold each year.

Alden Cohen, retired vice president of Chicago-based Packaging Dynamics Bagcraft Division—the largest airsickness-bag maker in the United States—said people love to take the bags. "It's like getting postcards in the hotel room." He said they are used for many other purposes, such as notepaper, eyeglass holders, finger puppets, and doggy bags.

Frank Norwick, curator for the San Francisco Airport Museum, claimed the bags became necessary around 1929, when half the passengers on flights would become ill. After a bag was filled, it was thrown out of the plane, an action frowned upon in today's world. Norwick also said that no inventor has come forward to admit inventing the little bag. Some people believe TWA flight attendants made up little containers while in flight back in the thirties. They saw a need for the barf bags and used materials they had on board. "This bag is nothing to sneeze at," commented a flight attendant after a passenger filled one. "Maybe to gag at, though."

> *If the Wright brothers were alive today, Wilbur would have to fire Orville to reduce costs.*
>
> —HERB KELLEHER,
> Southwest Airlines CEO

Off Airport Grounds

Busted

THE CAPTAIN WENT THROUGH FIRST OFFICERS like someone eating potato chips—one right after another. He was touchy, critical, nasty, and a braggart.

His favorite toy to boast about was his new black Porsche and how fast he drove it and how well he executed turns. During one flight, he told his two officers in the cockpit that after they landed later in Miami, he was taking it for a spin on Alligator Alley, a road that cuts through the Everglades from Fort Lauderdale to Naples, Florida.

As soon as the captain left the gate area, the first officer called the Florida Highway Patrol and said, "I want to report a drug dealer driving a new black Porsche. He's leaving the

Miami airport and driving west on Alligator Alley. The car is loaded with drugs."

The state police were grateful for the tip. The next day in the cockpit, the busted captain told his crew how he had been wrongfully pulled over by the state police on Alligator Alley. Based on an anonymous tip, they'd searched his car, practically dismantling it, he complained to them.

No one flinched as he retold the trauma of being pulled over by the police. He never talked much about his Porsche after that.

Tax Time

MOONLIGHTING AS A CERTIFIED PUBLIC ACCOUNTANT during tax time and flying can be "taxing." However, Captain Randall maintained his ability to do both.

One day, he seemed somewhat scatterbrained and anxious as he entered the office. Dressed in full uniform for his 4:30 P.M. flight, he hurriedly finished a tax return before leaving for the airport.

At 3:00 P.M., he realized he had misplaced his car keys, so the office staff joined in the hunt for them. After an hour of searching, they still couldn't find the keys. It was now 4:00 P.M.—thirty minutes before his flight was scheduled to take off. The airport was about thirty minutes away.

"Hey, no big deal!" Randall told them, "This happens all the time. Why do you think flights are delayed? The passengers have to wait for the driver." Then he picked up the phone and called a cab.

Smooth Shopper

GARY PHILLIPS, A THIRTY-FIVE-YEAR-OLD California civil engineer, purchased $3,150 worth of pudding at his local grocery store and at a discount bulk supermarket, and by ordering directly from Healthy Choice. Nobody called him "Puddin' Head" to his face, but if they did, he probably wouldn't have minded. All that pudding turned into free airline tickets worth several hundred thousand dollars.

Gary bought the pudding after he noticed an airline frequent-flyer promotion while grocery shopping one day.

For every ten UPC symbols turned in, 500 miles would be given. What made the deal even more attractive was the doubling of miles for all early entries. Standing in the aisle, "I did the math, and I realized this was a great deal," Gary recalled. By the time he finished buying pudding in various places, he had 12,150 cups of the creamy stuff.

Because he realized he could not eat it all, he donated all the pudding to local food pantries in the Davis, California, area. He also realized he would not have enough time to peel all the UPC symbols off the containers. Food pantry volunteers accomplished that project, so he was able to take advantage of the early entry and, thus, the double miles. It was a win-win situation because the food banks received the pudding and he was given an $815 tax write-off for the donation.

Gary won't be purchasing any plane tickets for quite a while. His initial investment of $3,150 was parlayed into approximately thirty-one round-trip flights to Europe, or forty-two trips to Hawaii, or twenty-one trips to Australia, or fifty trips to anywhere in the contiguous United States. He's glad he "did the math" in that grocery store aisle.

And this, ladies and gentlemen, is the very first Fokker airplane built in the world. The Dutch call it the mother Fokker.

—GUIDE
at Amsterdam's Schiphol Airport Museum

Late Can Be Great

AFTER A DELAYED FLIGHT and a missed connection, Tami Claybourne finally checked into her Phoenix hotel. Coincidentally, Rick Robbins was also checking into the same hotel after a harried day of air travel in the fall of 2000.

As they each registered, she started a conversation with him, he took the hint, and the next night they met for dinner. They had a wonderful dinner and talked until 4:00 A.M. (yes, talked), and he postponed his departure.

If she hadn't missed her flight and been late checking in, they would never have found each other. As fate would have it, he missed his flight the following day. But he didn't mind — he had found the woman of his dreams. Less than a year later, they were married.

Nuggets from Heaven

WHEN ALASKA AIRLINES DONATED FOUR FREE TICKETS to raffle off for Junior Achievement in Nome, Alaska, local author Lew Tobin suggested that the JA make it interesting by selling raffle tickets for frozen moose droppings, or nuggets. Each of the 3,000 nuggets would be numbered and then dropped from an airplane. The person whose numbered nugget came closest to landing on a target would win the Alaska Airlines tickets.

The Nome Rotary Club, the Civil Air Patrol, and the First National Bank of Anchorage printed the raffle tickets and planned the actual drop, while an employee of the Alaska Mining Association gathered 1,500 nuggets. Procuring the other half proved more difficult, so Tobin resorted to the Internet for assistance. By the middle of October, fresh and frozen nuggets arrived from all over the state. Eventually, 3,000 frozen moose droppings were packed and numbered at the local correctional center by the inmates.

The Federal Aviation Administration gave permission for the plane, a Cessna 180, to fly at only 1,000 feet above the target area, the parking lot next to the football stadium. Because of the configuration of the aircraft's door, a chute had to be devised in order to release the 3,000 nuggets. So Tobin constructed a "poop chute" from stovepipe sections, a metal hopper, and a damper. With bungee cords, he fastened the device between a seat and the plane door.

All went perfectly well on the practice run with 1,000 extra nuggets. However, for the real drop, the plastic bag holding the 3,000 nuggets caught the edge of the hopper. Wind forced the nuggets back into the plane, where they flew haphazardly through the cabin before they were dropped.

Thanks to the nugget drop, Nome raised $1,000 for the local Junior Achievement. Everyone had a great time working together and solving problems. The chute operator, a local teacher, returned to class where, he later recalled, "nuggets kept dropping out of my shirt."

The Unknown Salmon

IN 1997, A SALMON THAT ALLOWED itself to be caught by a hungry bald eagle unwittingly grounded a commercial airliner.

While swimming peacefully in an Alaskan river, the delectable-looking salmon suddenly was yanked out of the water by the talons of an eagle. As it swooped into the sky with its prey, the eagle suddenly spotted another giant bird heading straight for it. Without hesitation, the frightened eagle fled for its life, deciding to relinquish dinner rather than become dinner.

Talons flew open and the salmon fell through the air. Unable to navigate the sky, the fish then smashed into the cockpit window of the bigger "bird"—an Alaska Airlines Boeing 737. The plane had come from Juneau International Airport. The pilot had not witnessed the fishing expedition the eagle had been on earlier, but he did witness the fish hitting his windshield.

Concerned about the possible damage to the plane, the pilot of the Anchorage-bound jetliner made an emergency landing in Yakutat, 200 miles from its origin. Mechanics made a careful inspection of the plane's exterior, looking for dents, holes, or other structural damage. None was found. "They found a greasy spot with some scales on the windshield, but no damage," reported Paul Bowers, the Juneau airport manager.

The forty passengers on board were forced to cool their heels for approximately an hour during the inspection. Once the plane was pronounced airworthy, they reboarded and continued on to Anchorage. Because it was a short flight, no dinner service was provided, although many passengers had a hunger for Alaskan salmon.

The bizarre incident was recorded in aviation history as the first-ever midair collision between a commercial jetliner and a fish. The eagle apparently survived the trauma of losing its dinner, but the fish was never seen again and was presumed dead. Said the pilot, "I had a six-foot fish right in front of me, but he got away."

A Note To Readers

Do you have an outrageous but true air travel story you want to share? Did something happen to you as a passenger? Are you a pilot, flight attendant, or airline employee who wants to reveal a funny incident that happened to you in the air or at the terminal? If so, please tell us about it in a brief note. If we plan to use it for a second volume of *The Smile-High Club*, we will contact you first and we'll also guarantee anonymity if desired. All submissions become the property of the authors of this book. Please include your name and phone number and/or your e-mail address and send your true anecdote to:

The Wordsellers, Inc.
9 Poplar Forest
Fairview, NC 28730
wordseller@mindspring.com